Learn to Love Stress:

Turn stress into motivation, mental energy, emotional resilience, and happiness

by Sara Hansen

Ruskin Publishing

www.ruskinpublishing.co.uk

Editor: Justine Talbot

Cover Design: Sam Piper

Legal Notice:

The writer of this publication is not a medical professional and this book is not intended as a substitute for professional medical advice, diagnosis or treatment. The reader should consult a qualified health care provider with any questions relating to his/her health and particularly with respect to any symptoms that may require diagnosis or medical attention.

Introduction

Over the years, I have come to know that necessity often leads us to discover new information and to develop experience and expertise that we may not have needed otherwise. The information I have now is the result of years of reading and research following the diagnosis of a chronic pain condition for which there is no known cause, and as yet, no cure. So, I resolved to learn as much as I could about pain management, relaxation, and stress relief. I hope to pass this information on to you, as it has truly changed my life. I hope it will change yours, too.

If you're looking for a way to manage the stress in your life and turn it to your advantage; if you want to be more productive, organised, and happier – then you're reading the right book!

I would love for this book to be a little window into the fascinating and rapidly expanding area of stress and mindset research – introducing you to some new and mind-blowing ideas; moving you away from the 'stress-is-harmful' mindset and a little closer to the 'stress-is-beneficial' (or energising, motivating, exciting) and 'I'm-well-equipped-to-handle-this' mindset. After reading this book, you will hopefully find that although some stressful situations will be a challenge and stretch your limits, the knowledge you have gained will leave you feeling empowered and knowing that you are fully equipped to handle whatever comes your way (sometimes with help – that's what happens).

As you delve into the pages of this book, do not lose sight of the fact that however great any well-being, self-help or self-improvement book is, it is the efforts of the reader that make the book come to life! So, it is my hope that these few pages will resonate with you, but most importantly, will inspire you to act!

To get the most out of this book, I have designed a series of **FREE printable worksheets** which you can find here:

www.ruskinpublishing.co.uk/titles/

Table of contents

Chapter 1: What is Stress?

Keywords for this chapter
What is stress – good/bad stress
The hormonal cocktail
Athletes
Primary vs. secondary suffering

What are Stress, Worry, and Anxiety?

Stress! We hear about it all the time. Stress is blamed for headaches, muscle tension, sleep problems, anxiety, depression, heart disease, obesity... The list is endless! But is it really that bad for you? How can you avoid it? Should you even try? Or could it actually work for you and bring deeper meaning, motivation, and excitement back into your life?

Perhaps it all depends on your definition of stress – is it feeling rushed between your appointments for school, work, or a date with your boyfriend? Is it a job interview, packing for holidays, or moving house? Is it getting divorced? Or would you say that someone could feel excitement going through each of these situations?

Stress is difficult to define, because what is stressful for one could be a source of enjoyment for another. However, it can *generally* be defined as being under excessive emotional or mental pressure. In moments like these, the body returns to its natural 'fight or flight' (or sometimes freeze) response, triggered by increased levels of various stress hormones, such as adrenaline and cortisol. In a typical stress response, you might experience a pounding heartbeat, quickened breathing or excessive perspiration. Your body will react by constricting blood vessels – a response which could potentially lead to cardiovascular issues.

1

And what about worry and anxiety? Worrying engages your thinking brain — mostly your prefrontal cortex — which also deals with problem-solving and planning. Anxiety shows in a more physical way and engages the parts of your brain dealing with fear. Both worry and anxiety are natural to humankind. They are our brain's way of learning from past experiences and preventing the same things from happening again by making connections with their possible causes. They engage the same areas in your brain as fear and stress do, and thus trigger the same stress response and release of stress hormones. We could say that anxiety is a physical/bodily response to natural worry about an upcoming event or a situation for which we believe we are not well-enough equipped. It is the belief that we are unable to cope with challenging situations that increase our heart rate, give us sweaty palms and often prevent us from seeing objectively what lies ahead.

Anxiety and stress are both very real physical and emotional responses to events that are perceived as dangerous or intimidating. However, it seems the impact of stress and anxiety on our health is not due to their external factors, but largely due to our internal neuro-processing, which is ultimately affected by our belief systems.

If you have been suffering from stress, anxiety, or even pain for a while and have been through the system with doctors, therapists etc., chances are that you are looking for anything you can do to help yourself. This book will not help you if you expect someone else to fix you or your life on your behalf. It won't help you if you think that there is an easy, ready-to-use solution such as a winning lottery ticket or magic pill. This is not to say that there isn't a place for medical professionals in the management of severe anxiety, stress, or pain — there absolutely is — in this book, you will find very practical methods you can implement right now which can help you to feel better, live better, improving your life both physically and psychologically.

In 2011, a study of 30,000 Americans showed that high stress increases the risk of death by 43%.[1] Shockingly, this was only the case amongst those who already believed that the stress was bad for them! It had no impact at all on those who didn't believe that stress negatively affected their health. How is this possible?

You have in your hands a short guide to turning the effects of stress and anxiety upside-down and inside-out for good. We will introduce you to the recent body of research which will help to balance your view of stress and teach you to look at it optimistically. By priming your brain to view stressful situations in a positive way – in a way that is helpful to you and your situation – you can redefine your thinking and response pathways.

"If you can manage to interpret your body's response to the situation as positive, as a call to action, you are likely to thrive."[2]

"Research shows that around 85% of the time things turned out better than people feared, and they handled them better than they thought they would."[3] So here we go. **There is no such thing as good**

[1] Keller, A., Litzelman, K., Wisk, L. E., Maddox, T., Cheng, E. R., Creswell, P. D., & Witt, W. P. (2012). Does the Perception that Stress Affects Health Matter? The Association with Health and Mortality. *Health Psychology : Official Journal of the Division of Health Psychology, American Psychological Association, 31*(5), 677–684. http://doi.org/10.1037/a0026743

[2] Beilock, S. (2011) Choke: *What the Secrets of the Brain Reveal About Getting It Right When You Have To.* New York: Simon & Schuster

[3] Leahy, R. L. (2009). *Anxiety free: Unravel your fears before they unravel you.* Carlsbad, CA: Hay House.

stress or bad stress. Only our perception of it makes it so. So let's talk about the effects of stress on our physical and psychological wellbeing.

Good Stress/Bad Stress

As I have already mentioned, I will talk about stress, worry and anxiety as similar terms, as they often trigger the same or very similar reactions in the body.

However, for dealing with severe anxiety, please contact your medical professional (GP, mental health support, counsellor) and discuss with them how the principles outlined in this book can help complement your medical treatment.

Why would I take an optimistic approach to stress?

I have been suffering from various levels of chronic pain over the past five years (bear with me, this is not going to be a depressing read). This affected both my work and family life, as I was never able to find out what caused my pain and whether it would ever get better. The pain was accompanied by loss of self-confidence, fear of losing work, stress and anxiety, and grief about what I once could do and what I may not be able to do in the future.

I have been through numerous courses of medication, physiotherapy, cognitive behaviour therapy, pain management training and a course in mindful meditation. All of these have been great and helped to some extent – some better than others (which I will address in a moment) but I kept being thrown back, or one could say I kept throwing myself into despair over my future. In this state of mind, any tiny hassle in my life could bring me down (no milk in the fridge, weeds in the garden, missed bus). Seriously, you would have thought

I had bigger fish to fry, such as the fact that I struggled to hold my newborn for more than 5 minutes due to the pain in my arms.

You would have thought that suffering from often severe pain would change my perception of what matters and what doesn't. I had some really hard times but I also had some amazing times. I found myself feeling best during the times I was super-busy, or when I spent time with friends and family or on holiday. Some social gatherings and holidays, however, made me feel more stressed, causing me to suffer both mentally and physically. Between that, and seeing and understanding that others suffered more or were in more dire circumstances, I began to question myself.

I began to question the nature of suffering and how it related to the stress, pain, and anxiety I felt. I could see that some of my friends were not suffering as much as I did, even though their medical condition, pain, or life situation was much worse (terminal condition, death of a spouse, bankruptcy, loss of job). I could also see that situations I found stressful and taxing were not stressful for others and vice versa.

I started questioning the differences between us. Why did our perceptions of what is stressful and what it means to be stressed differ so greatly from person to person? Why did it affect some people much less? Doesn't stress work in the same way for everybody? Why were there some days that I felt really excited about my work and others when I felt stressed, even though the work and deadlines were the same? Did it actually have anything to do with my pain, which side of the bed I rolled out of in the morning, or was it my general mindset and where I focussed my attention that was letting me down?

I probably would still be looking for the answers had I not stumbled upon a TED Talk by Kelly McGonigal, which has changed my life. [4] It jettisoned me on a journey of research and learning as well as self-discovery and improvement. It helped me ask the right questions and it really helped me put into perspective all I've learned through my journey over the past five years – an experience I would really like to share with you.

In the last two decades, research into stress has been blossoming. Studies have investigated the effects of stress on behaviour, physical and mental health, as well as its impact on the workplace and global economy. The research has been plagued by difficulties in defining stress, as it really does vary greatly from one person to another, and affects people from all walks of life. Someone might find shopping stressful; another may be stressed by being at home with the baby on their own; others may fear giving presentations or jumping out of a plane; yet others will love and revel in all these situations. Unsurprisingly, given the vast differences between people, the research has brought to light some surprises.

As mentioned previously, in 2011, a study of nearly 30,000 Americans showed that high levels of stress increased the risk of premature death by 43%.[5] Whilst these are shocking statistics, it turned out that **this was only the case amongst those who already believed that the**

---

[4] McGonigal, K. (2013, September). Kelly McGonigal: How to make stress your best friend [video file]. Retrieved from https://www.ted.com/talks/kelly_mcgonigal_how_to_make_stress_your_friend

[5] Keller, A., Litzelman, K., Wisk, L. E., Maddox, T., Cheng, E. R., Creswell, P. D., & Witt, W. P. (2012). Does the Perception that Stress Affects Health Matter? The Association with Health and Mortality. *Health Psychology : Official Journal of the Division of Health Psychology, American Psychological Association, 31*(5), 677–684. http://doi.org/10.1037/a0026743

stress was bad for their health! It had no impact at all on those who experienced high levels of stress but didn't believe that it had any negative effects on their health.

Although this study had some limitations, the researchers estimated that over 20,000 Americans annually could be facing premature death thanks to this damaging belief (based on the numbers collected over 9 years). Despite the imperfect nature of the study, it sparked a lot of interest amongst medical researchers, and has since been followed by a body of new research that explores how a person's mindset (core beliefs about how the world works) predicts and influences longevity, happiness, and mental as well as physical health.[6, 7, 8]

So the physiological and psychological effects of stress are significant and getting cosy with your stress – not resisting it – can lead to excitement, joy, and courage in the face of challenge in a similar way to the above experiment. However, for this belief to become deep-rooted and long-lasting without needing your conscious attention, you need at least a minimal understanding of what stress and anxiety are and how they can be affected by your mindset, amongst many other things. This will not only help you choose the best strategies for

---

[6] Levy BR, Slade MD, Kunkel SR, Klas SV. Longevity increased by positive self-perceptions of aging. J Pers Soc Psychol. 2002;83(3):261–270. [PubMed]

[7] Barefoot JC, Maynard KE, Beckham JC, et al. Trust, health, and longevity. J Behav Med 1998;21:517–26. doi:10.1023/A:1018792528008 [PubMed]

[8] Crum, A., Salovey, P. & Achor, S. (2013). Rethinking Stress: The Role of Mindsets in Determining the Stress Response. *Journal of Personality and Social Psychology*, 104(4), 716-733.
https://mbl.stanford.edu/sites/default/files/crum_rethinkingstress_jpsp_2013_0.pdf

you, but will also help you stick with them throughout your life – and not just when the proverbial hits the fan.

Because stress and anxiety are so frequent in our lives nowadays, befriending stress and using it to your advantage can have a massive transformative effect on your life, for your physical as well as psychological well-being.

The Hormonal Cocktail of Stress

When your body is under stress or in danger, either perceived or real, the hypothalamus in your brain signals to your adrenal glands to release stress-related hormones, namely adrenaline and cortisol. This sets off a reaction in your body which, from an evolutionary perspective, used to tell you to get out of danger. Many people think of this as the 'fight or flight' response. However, it was also meant to help you think quickly, heal, and grow. The physical stress response (the release of hormones as we discuss below) is not a simple process and one cannot say it is either good or bad. Let's take a closer look.

Adrenaline is responsible for increasing your heart rate and elevating your blood pressure, as well as boosting your energy supplies. **Cortisol** helps with improving brain function as well as tissue repair, through directing more sugars and fat into your bloodstream. However, cortisol also inhibits non-essential processes such as the reproductive and digestive systems, as well as growth processes. Let's face it, these are of no use to you when running away from a lion! However, this effect of cortisol may not seem so useful nowadays, as it used to happen when facing dangerous, life-threatening predators.

To counterbalance this hormonal reaction, our stress response also has a built-in countermeasure under the guise of the hormones **oxytocin** and **DHEA** (Dehydroepiandrosterone). Oxytocin is a

8

neurohormone, which means that it affects both our psychology and physiology. It enhances empathy, makes us seek out relationships and support in times of need, and makes us want to help people we care about.

However, these hormones do not only affect our brain and how we behave, but also how our heart recovers from stress. Oxytocin acts as a natural anti-inflammatory, which helps blood vessels to stay relaxed. Your heart also has receptors for this hormone, which aids in heart cell regeneration from any stress-induced damage (McGonigal, 2015).[9]

In her Ted Talk, McGonigal says, "So when you reach out to others under stress, either to seek support or to help someone else, you release more of this hormone, your stress response becomes healthier, and you actually recover faster from stress."[10]

DHEA, a neurosteroid hormone synthesised from cholesterol and secreted by the adrenal glands, is always present in times of stress. It counteracts some of the effects of cortisol to help with recovery from stress. More importantly, it helps our brain learn and grow stronger in a similar way to how testosterone improves the strength of your body after physical exercise and stress.

Another important neurochemical produced at times of stress is **Brain-Derived Neurotrophic Factor – BDNF**. This one helps your brain

---

[9] McGonigal, K. (2015) *The upside of stress: Why stress is good for you (and how to get good at it)*. London, United Kingdom: Vermilion.

[10] McGonigal, K. (2013, September). Kelly McGonigal: How to make stress your best friend [video file]. Retrieved from https://www.ted.com/talks/kelly_mcgonigal_how_to_make_stress_your_friend

grow (learn) and protects against the effects of ageing on your thinking abilities.

All of the above hormones are very important to our body function and none of them is either good or bad. The sticking point seems to be not only how long or how often these are in your bloodstream, but also the ratio of these hormones to one another, therefore influencing the long-term consequences of stress on you. Surprisingly, you can affect these by what you do and how you do it (for example by exercise, mindfulness, habits etc.), but also, by your core beliefs – your so-called 'mindset'.

A study conducted by researchers at Harvard University (Jamieson, Nock, & Mendes, 2012)[11] found that if students during a stress test viewed the usual physical signs (sweaty palms, fast heartbeat, butterflies in stomach) as positive, energising, and as preparation to meet the challenge, their blood vessels did not constrict and their hearts pumped as if they were experiencing joy and courage. They managed to decrease the negative impact on their cardiovascular systems! Not only that, but they also performed better in their test!

The physical response of the students changed because they were primed to see their physical stress response as helpful (the 'stress-is-enhancing' mindset). They were told that their pounding heart was preparing them for action and that faster breathing would improve their performance by increasing the delivery of oxygen to the brain. This meant that they stopped resisting and feeling worried about the

---

[11] Jamieson, J. P., Nock, M. K., & Mendes, W. B. (2012). Mind over matter: Reappraising arousal improves cardiovascular and cognitive responses to stress. *Journal of Experimental Psychology: General, 141*(3), 417–422. doi:10.1037/a0025719

effects of stress. Their bodies, in turn, changed their physiological reaction to stress in accordance with this belief.

This concept doesn't only work on stressed people. Jamieson and colleagues (2013)[12] have shown that the method used in the research also helps people with very real anxieties, such as those suffering from social anxiety disorder. This disorder can affect many areas of people's lives, such as going to work, social or family gatherings, public speaking, or just plain shopping and asking where the toilets are. It can bring on feelings such as 'Everyone can see how nervous I am. I did something stupid. I can't talk to people. I look and feel stupid'; it can lead to social isolation and even result in full-blown panic attacks. The above study showed that during a stress test, people suffering from social anxiety disorder benefitted from a mindset intervention in the same way as people who did not suffer from anxiety. They showed the same increase in confidence and improvement in performance as those without anxiety disorder!

Even though medical professionals, scientists, and journalists have been scaring us for a long time by explaining the dangers of stress (probably hoping that we will do something about the stress in our lives), it may have had an undesired effect. Their message scared us, and you know what happens when you're scared? You try to run away or avoid the scary situation, but there are some situations that you simply cannot avoid. Sadly, it's often the case that the more you resist something, the more it will persist in your life. The more you see the messages about stress being dangerous, the more likely you are to

---

[12] Jeremy P. Jamieson, Matthew K. Nock, and Wendy Berry Mendes. Changing the Conceptualization of Stress in Social Anxiety Disorder: Affective and Physiological Consequences. Clinical Psychological Science, April 8, 2013 DOI: 10.1177/2167702613482119

feel stressed and worried or scared, thereby perpetuating the situation. This perceived danger then becomes a self-fulfilling prophecy. It is like being strapped to a heart rate monitor and being told that you will receive a painful electric shock if your heart rate goes up. Well, what do you think will happen?

I'd like to stress (no pun intended!) that I am in no way saying that stress – especially long-term or an exceptionally high level of stress – is not damaging. There are pieces of research that demonstrate the damage it can cause to your brain (the part that regulates your stress hormones – hippocampus) and heart (atherosclerosis – certainly in monkeys)[13] as well as it compromising your immune system.[14] **However, these scary effects (that may have many other underlying causes as well) are not irreversible.**

Often, you cannot control what stress you are exposed to, but physically, fight-or-flight isn't the only response in your repertoire; neither is the avoidance of stress or anxiety. The way you react to a stressful situation can vary significantly. It can be the '**excite and delight**' response skydivers have when jumping out of planes (giving them a rush, thanks to a mix of endorphins, adrenaline, testosterone, and dopamine); '**challenge response**', which gives you energy to perform under pressure (athletes and public speakers) and also increases the levels of DHEA and helps your heart and brain recover from stress; or the '**tend and befriend**' response which makes

---

[13] Stress: Portrait of a killer. (2008). Top Documentary Films. Available here: http://topdocumentaryfilms.com/stress-portrait-of-a-killer/

[14] Segerstrom, S. C., & Miller, G. E. (2004). Psychological Stress and the Human Immune System: A Meta-Analytic Study of 30 Years of Inquiry. *Psychological Bulletin, 130*(4), 601–630. http://doi.org/10.1037/0033-2909.130.4.601

you social and better able to engage with your family, friends, and community, resulting in higher levels of oxytocin.

The good news here is that you can retrain your brain and influence which stress response you go through. It isn't easy and it isn't a quick fix, but with practice, you can learn to view regular stressful situations in your life as motivating challenges. You will draw your energy from them and use them as opportunities to learn and grow. This, in turn, will help your brain downregulate your stress response on a neurochemical level.

Why you Should Become Friends with Stress

Motivation, energy, and meaning

I'm sure you've lived through a day at work where there were no deadlines – nothing exciting, just slogging through the day-to-day routine. Do these days make you want to be brave and amazing at what you do? Do they make you want to go the extra mile? Do they bring a spring to your step? Do these days make you feel stressed? I expect the answer is no, to all the above.

How can you appreciate and value what you do if you don't have a deadline or an expectation of how well you should perform? How do you know when you've done extremely well? Research suggests that getting rid of stress altogether will decrease motivation and the energy we feel when we deal with day-to-day life. Heavy pressure kills creativity, makes people unhappy and can lead to burn-out. Low-pressure, however, results in a lack of meaning or pride in your achievements.[15] It seems that low-to-medium pressure would be the way to go, if we learn to handle it in a positive manner and view it as a great challenge to which we CAN measure up. After all, our body does give us the resources (heartbeat, oxygen, glucose) and the ability comes from our brain (through emotional resilience).

By being able to decide which stress is meaningful to you and where you want to focus your attention, you are empowering yourself to take back control of your life. Take your work situation, for example. You might have a job where your routine is extremely predictable and somewhat monotonous by nature – and if that is the case, you'll either enjoy it or feel very unmotivated and disengaged. On the other hand, you could be working in a very demanding job, with lots of stress attached to the deadlines and even people with whom you work. However, if you attach a meaning to your stressor – in this case, work (or any other chore) – you are more likely to be satisfied with your work. If you realise the value of your work and why you are doing it, you are less likely to suffer the negative effects of stress attached to it.

So, whatever you do, think about what meaning it brings to your life.

Do you head off to work each day so that your family can enjoy luxuries in life, or to pay for a home for them? Do you go because it gets you amongst like-minded people, gives you experience or acts as the stepping stone to a better career? If you can ascribe meaning to anything you do, whatever value you can find in it, doing it becomes

---

[15] Amabile, T. & Kramer, S. (2011). The Progress Principle: Using Small Wins to Ignite Joy, Engagement, and Creativity at Work. Harvard, Massachusetts: Harvard Business Review Press.

less of a chore and more of a resilience training – and possibly even an enjoyable one.

If you feel trapped or stressed in your job or any other situation, you can change how you think about it by job crafting.[16] You can make it into, or as close to as possible to, what you need or want it to be. You can do this by focussing on reshaping how you do and think about your tasks, as well as your work relationships, or the way you use your knowledge.

- Tasks – If you're in any position to do so, change the set of responsibilities that are prescribed by your formal job description and spend more time, attention, and energy on the tasks that you enjoy (e.g. new work is available in customer service and you enjoy communicating with customers via social media – so do more of it!).

- People – Spend your work time liaising with colleagues that you value and build good relationships with them. Take them out to lunch; invite them over for a games night; or join them on an outing. It doesn't have to be expensive.

- Purpose – Assign a deeper meaning to your job description. For example, cleaners working in hospitals can see themselves as ambassadors of the hospital and an essential part of making patients better.

---

[16] Berg, J. M., Dutton, J. E., & Wrzesniewski, A. (2013). Job crafting and meaningful work. In B. J. Dik, Z. S. Byrne & M. F. Steger (Eds.), Purpose and meaning in the workplace (pp. 81-104). Washington, DC: American Psychological Association.

If you would like to try this from home, you can try our free printable "1.1 Job Crafting" (remember, all resources can be downloaded via www.ruskinpublishing.co.uk/titles/).

In the job that pays my bills (I'm not the only writer that needs one, I hope!) I often forget the value of my input and the difference it makes. It is difficult to ascribe meaning in those times until I look at my goal more deeply. What value does it bring to my life? What value does it bring to the lives of people around me? I find the following questions helpful at this point:

1) What goal is this helping me achieve? (It brings financial benefits and makes visiting my family abroad possible.)

2) Is this in any way meaningful to my life? (Yes, it helps me socialise and bring up my child to know and understand where I came from.)

3) Is this challenging me and teaching me anything? (Oh, yes! It's teaching me patience and widening my horizons.)

4) Will this help me in the future? (Yes, through all the above, the experience, and the social network I built.)

5) Is my output helping anybody else? (Yes, it's helping my colleagues as well as my hubby, who doesn't have to be a sole earner in the family.)

You might find meaning in knowing that your job helps to provide the basic needs for your family, as well as finances to enjoy your hobbies. If you work for a charity, belief or ideology may be the most important factor to you. Perhaps you find meaning in being able to help others advance and learn (I like to think that training documentation written by me helps my colleagues advance and get better jobs). Art-oriented people may take pride in seeing their work displayed and admired.

I deeply believe that if we don't care, we won't feel stressed. An 'easier' life is not necessarily a healthier or happier one. Things we care about are bound to make us feel precious about them and it is important to notice the difference; pay attention to areas you value and shift your focus away from those that aren't worth worrying about. Challenges exist to be overcome and challenging yourself will make you stronger. How do I know? Let's look at those who do it on a daily basis.

Who uses stress effectively

What's the difference between high performing athletes and the rest of us? **Athletes use their physical responses to stress to improve their performance. They stress their bodies on purpose** (hint: we SHOULD exercise regularly) to prepare themselves for handling pressure and because they do this, and because they view the challenge positively, their brain and body handles the experience in a more natural way. They revel in their beating heart and use their excitement to fuel their performance. Even though they are under a lot of pressure, and experience all or most of the physical reactions to stress (elevated heart rate, blood pressure, faster breathing, surges of energy and adrenaline) as well as pain, they rarely, if at all, consider their experience as suffering.

Let's look at a specific example: Serena Williams is one of the greatest tennis players of all time. When she won the Wimbledon 2016 tournament, she equalled Steffi Graf's record of 22 Grand Slam titles – no mean feat! Serena has been world number 1 for almost all of the last six years. However, things have not always been rosy for her. A lot of people forget that she had a terrible, severe injury that sent her down the world rankings by almost 200 places. Even so, she came back to the top and will surely go down in history as one of greatest sportspeople of all time. How can someone who suffered such a brutal and painful fall from the top get back to where they were?

Well, not only is Serena used to deliberately stressing her body, she also has the appropriate mindset to go with the physical exertion. When she starts a pre-match practice, her heart will begin to pump a bit faster; her blood pressure will increase. Rather than seeing these things as bad (because some people would want to stay calm before a major event), she sees these things as necessary and beneficial. Faster breathing coupled with raised blood pressure and heart rate sends more oxygen around your body. Adrenaline flow increases. These physical responses help all humans, not just athletes like Serena, to perform under pressure. We *want* these effects to happen. They aren't bad; they help us if we choose to see them as necessary and desirable things! Perhaps we should also learn to treat our daily lives at work or home like a tennis match?

What I have described is the main difference between a person able to use stress in a positive manner to their advantage and one who suffers from stress. The keyword here is suffering. As in pain, there is **primary and secondary suffering.**[17] Primary suffering is the actual physical response (pain, heart rate, fast breathing) and secondary suffering is how we think about it or what meaning we assign to it. The way you reframe your view of the stress you experience – either

---

[17] Burch, V. (2005). One moment at a time. Retrieved February 12, 2017, from Breathworks-Mindfulness, http://www.breathworks-mindfulness.org.uk/articles/one-moment-at-a-time

as potentially advantageous, exciting, or energising – will have a massive impact on the rest of your life.

As we said before, it is the prolonged exposure to stress and anxiety that can be damaging. So why don't elite athletes just burn out? Why do they live longer than the general population and suffer fewer cardiovascular-related deaths?[18, 19]

This is most likely because the best performing athletes also make the best use of micro-breaks, a method that teaches their bodies and minds to relax in order to avoid the burnout of continuous stress. They turn their stress on and off.[20] Again, tennis is a great example, because there are several small breaks throughout what could be a few hours of physically stressful exertion (not to mention the mental focus required). We can easily apply this to our daily lives. Even the busiest of people take several short breaks throughout a typical day – you still need to go to the toilet, grab a drink, grab some lunch and commute. These are opportune moments for a micro-break.

What you do with these breaks is supremely important. If we are to be energetic, engaged individuals, capable of performing when we need to, then we need to maximise our opportunity for recovery. You

---

[18] Teramoto, M., & Bungum, T. J. (2010). Mortality and longevity of elite athletes. *Journal of Science and Medicine in Sport*, *13*(4), 410–416. doi:10.1016/j.jsams.2009.04.010; retrieved Feb 12, 2017; from: https://www.researchgate.net/profile/Timothy_Bungum/publication/26337602

[19] Lemez, S., & Baker, J. (2015). Do elite athletes live longer? A systematic review of mortality and longevity in elite athletes. *Sports Medicine - Open*, *1*(1). doi:10.1186/s40798-015-0024-x; retrieved Feb 12, 2017; from: http://www.ncbi.nlm.nih.gov/pmc/articles/PMC4534511/

[20] Waitzkin, J. (2008). *The art of learning: an inner journey to optimal performance*. New York: Simon & Schuster

could spend a few minutes mindfully focussing on your breath, soaking up the sunshine (or rain), stroking your dog, or even watching a happy monkey video (as long as you are not stressed that your boss will catch you). Yes, pets are good for us.[21] Being with animals can help regulate stress, but research shows that even watching a 60-second video with cute animals will decrease your heart rate and blood pressure and help you to ward off the effects of stress and anxiety.[22]

Please note that watching a home video of your dog destroying the furniture in your house while you are trying to work would in my eyes not be considered relaxing unless a) you fancied new furniture anyway, hence leaving the dog to it; or b) you can share the video with your colleagues and laugh about it all the way home ;-)

Let's bring this discussion back to the topic of athletes. I would also ask you to ponder the game side of elite athletes' lives. It is their living. If they fail, they might lose their current livelihood, prestige, and maybe also their fans. But then the top athletes diversify into many businesses. You could argue that their main occupation as an athlete is treating their life as a game and perhaps this is also a reason why they can't be affected by stress so much. Why don't we turn this around and make our life – or as much of it as possible into a game? Are you stressed about getting up at 5AM? Give yourself 5 points for every time you manage it this week. Did you do it at least 5 times?

[21] Wells, D. L. (2009), The Effects of Animals on Human Health and Well-Being. *Journal of Social Issues*, 65: 523–543. doi:10.1111/j.1540-4560.2009.01612.x

[22] Wells, D. L. (2005), The effect of videotapes of animals on cardiovascular responses to stress. Stress and Health, 21: 209–213. doi:10.1002/smi.1057

Reward yourself with something you value: a new book, a cinema trip, a pizza night, or a relaxing massage or bath.

What to Appreciate about Stress

I am convinced, and hopefully now you are too, that we need some stress (or our physical response to it) for motivation and doing our best! We cannot, and do not want to get rid of stress completely, but the one thing we need to change in order to be and feel well is our reaction to and interpretation of the physical and emotional states associated with stress. We must change our minds about stress and learn to embrace it.

You can follow me through learning to think about your mindset, realise your values and take control. You will learn to implement structure, happiness practices, and rituals in your life. Through building emotional resilience and better relationships you will engage oxytocin to the fullest. These strategies will bring motivation, energy and more meaning to your life. I will then provide you with further strategies and resources with which you can enhance your practice and you will have access to a whole section of resources available online as well.

By the end of this book, I hope you will feel somewhat like an amazing athlete dealing with your day-to-day life. You will learn to make stress work for you. I want you to feel the excitement and motivation, the blood pumping through your veins and heart, I want you to feel alive! Your journey will begin by getting friendly and very cosy with stress, without the physical and psychological costs.

These strategies have been used by everyone from college students, stay-at-home mums and new fathers to world-class athletes, public speakers, and high-performance CEOs. If you're reading this book, then we can safely assume that you're open to changing your mind about stress, or at least trying to manage it differently. Perhaps you want a better quality of life, to be able to react appropriately and have enough mental energy to cope with everyday struggles, and especially when it comes to life-changing events such as the birth of a first child, loss of a loved one, a business collapsing, or a divorce.

I fully accept that not every trauma or stressful event in your life can be managed away by positivity or other strategies. However, having access to and building up our emotional resilience, our support network, and our ability to be happy (it really is a skill that can be practised), I firmly believe that we will be better equipped to deal with all that life can throw at us and not just survive, but really thrive.

Summary of Chapter 1

- Stress is the feeling of being under too much pressure.

- We can have a 'typical' psychological response to it, e.g. flight, fight, or freeze; as well as a physical response such as a pounding heart, sweating, breathing faster, shaking hands etc.

- There is a hormonal cocktail that kicks into action when under stress.

- There is no such thing as good stress or bad stress; it is only our perception that makes it so.

- You can retrain your brain and your response to stress so it energises and motivates you.

- You can use the same methods as elite athletes to enhance your everyday life.

Chapter 2: Mindset and Vision

Keywords for this chapter
Mindsets
Vision
Inner optimist/inner pessimist
Goals and willpower

What is Mindset?

We have mentioned mindset before but what exactly is it and how does it work? Why is it critically important? Mindset is a term used to describe your beliefs and overall attitude toward your circumstances. It influences what you think about the world and how it works, which, in turn, affects the way you behave. It is a set of beliefs based on our past experiences as well as the expectations of the culture in which we live.

Many people in western cultures feel stressed about juggling work/kids/life, applying for college, a new job, or a multitude of other things. They transfer these feelings onto their children, and they readily attribute their physical symptoms to stress because that is the norm. Take, for example, going for a job interview. Most people will feel anxious about going for an interview or applying for a new job and they'll often tell you all about it. Perhaps you're in the middle of preparing for your own job interview. Perhaps people have told you it's stressful. You might feel a bit excited, but you're also anxious and thinking to yourself, "So this is what stress feels like." You've automatically associated what you've been told with your own nervousness, thus enhancing the negative effects of stress on your physical and psychological wellbeing.

However, in high-stress situations, your brain automatically attributes emotions to circumstances at face-value and the brain can get it wrong. For instance, your brain can make you feel like you are in love because your first date involved a roller coaster ride. In this scenario, you associated the scary and exhilarating ride with the feeling of being in love. To address this, you cannot attribute a static connection between your physical symptoms and emotions. Our general life's circumstances give us these generalisations, but you can use this flexibility of your brain to your advantage. Not only can you label your emotions in the heat of the moment or depths of despair as a coping mechanism, you can re-label your emotions as well as physical symptoms through mindset interventions. You can access www.ruskinpublishing.co.uk/titles/ and use worksheet: "2.1 Labelling Emotions" and "2.2 ACT on Stress".

"The way we verbalize and think about our feelings helps to construct the way we actually feel."[23] This does not mean you can reinvent and re-imagine every negative event in your life. The way you perceive things is, as mentioned above, largely influenced by outside factors as well: the culture you live in, your physical situation, and your genes. Despite experiencing circumstances you cannot change, you can flex your mindset and it will go a long way, surprisingly, transforming your view (and the feel) of many things in life.

Think about public speaking. Most people are worried or even outright scared when asked to speak publicly or present ideas to their superiors. However, research shows that challenging this fear through the use of simple strategies such as positive self-talk ('I'm

---

[23] Brooks, A. W. (2014). Get excited: Reappraising pre-performance anxiety as excitement. *Journal of Experimental Psychology: General*, *143*(3), 1144–1158. doi:10.1037/a0035325

excited') or messages such as 'get excited' completely transform the effect of the stress and anxiety you feel. They don't stop your stress or anxiety – you will still feel your sweaty palms and faster heartbeat. However, by re-labelling your feelings, you will take control of the opportunity and perform better (as well as helping your brain release more oxytocin, DHEA and BDNF). You will be perceived as a more persuasive speaker[24] and this success will, in turn, help you become more confident in other areas, either at work or at home. It will become possible to take on more challenges and you will be able to transfer your opportunity or challenge your mindset in other areas of life: "I am excited about this and my excitement is contagious as well as energising." This change in mindset will have a wide-ranging, long-term impact, snowballing over time, if you are ready to transfer this skill into other areas of your life and practise it often. Remember to use the worksheet "2.2 ACT on Stress".

Types of Mindset – Fixed vs. Growth Mindset

Mindset isn't only about positive or negative attitudes. It's also about change, belonging and how capable or influential you believe yourself to be. Chances are that when you went through school, you received praise for your achievements at some time or other. Both your teachers and parents may have used positive encouragement to help you to move forward in your education. But how did they do it? Consider this: imagine two pupils working on a project at school. Both have finished the project successfully, albeit at different times perhaps, and the teacher tells each one something slightly different:

---

[24] Brooks, A. W. (2014). Ibid.

1) "Well done! You are *so* clever! What a great talent you have"; and

2) "Well done! You have worked really hard and persevered. I hope you feel good and proud of yourself."

You see here that the first feedback supports the idea of talent – something innate that you either do or don't have, a concept that Carol Dweck referred to as 'fixed mindset'.[25] It suggests that you have what you were born with and regardless of what you do, this is what you will always be/have. On the other hand, the second statement supports the development of a 'growth mindset' and with it, the possibility that you can change, improve, learn from others, and work hard to grow, improve yourself and develop your abilities.

No matter how fashionable it is currently to say that you have a 'growth mindset', especially in business settings, you most likely have a 'fixed mindset' too – at least in some areas. You may have a growth mindset at work (you believe you can get a better position if you perform well) but when it comes to your personal life, you may be unable to believe that you can change the situation you live in, progress, or do anything about your struggles. So, for a day or two, think about which aspects of your life you value and consider what you believe – do you believe that your current situation is a fixed one that can't be changed, or do you consider yourself to be able to contribute, improve and grow from where you are now? Can you

---

[25] Dweck, C. (2016, January 13). What having a "Growth Mindset" actually means. Retrieved February 2, 2017, from Managing yourself, https://hbr.org/2016/01/what-having-a-growth-mindset-actually-means

challenge yourself about what you really think? Try this printable worksheet: "2.3 Challenge Your Mindset".

Let's re-cap. 'Stress-is-harmful' is a mindset – a belief that isn't fixed and can be changed by a mindset intervention (worksheet "2.4 Mindset Intervention"). Our beliefs have a huge influence on our wellbeing, both physical and psychological. This is not only due to our hormones and how we approach on-the-spot challenges, but it also has a lot do to with self-fulfilling prophecies; the stories we tell ourselves. We know self-fulfilling prophecies work (although not necessarily why), especially if they relate to our self-perception and health. Research from Yale found that "older individuals with more positive self-perceptions of aging [...] lived 7.5 years longer than those with less positive self-perceptions of aging."[26]

One of the theories about why self-fulfilling prophecies/mindsets work is that if you believe that you cannot control or influence a certain area of your life, you might subconsciously stop trying. You might turn to bad habits to soothe your aches, pains, stresses and anxieties – to make yourself feel better and get a hit of a dopamine (that's what happens when you smoke a cigarette – it makes you feel good even though you know it isn't good for you). If you believe that your effort doesn't make any difference and that your suffering is meaningless, it is very disempowering. Beliefs that are not empowering erode your willpower and motivation to be your best. These beliefs deserve to be challenged, argued with and stomped on!

---

[26] Levy, B. R., Slade, M. D., Kunkel, S. R., & Kasl, S. V. (2002). Longevity increased by positive self-perceptions of aging. *Journal of Personality and Social Psychology*, *83*(2), 261–270. doi:10.1037/0022-3514.83.2.261 (freely available here: https://www.researchgate.net/publication/11232977)

Mindset Change – Case Study

It could only take an hour or a single book (hopefully) to achieve a significant change in how you feel and consequently in what you do. David Yeager (a mindset researcher at the University of Texas at Austin) ran a mindset intervention[27] as an experimental part of his research. His conclusion was that a brief intervention, teaching students that people can change, led to the students showing less negativity towards social adversity and "... 8 months later, reported lower overall stress and physical illness. They also achieved better academic performance over the year."

How did they do it? How did they change the mindset of these pupils, who had come from a significant place of disadvantage, from families with a very low income and attending an underperforming school where they didn't feel safe? They began by first presenting these adolescents with an article introducing the idea of personal growth. The article emphasised the concept that people can change; that who you are now is not who you will be later in life; that how people see you now will be different from their opinion of you in the future – and you won't be labelled as a 'nerd' forever. Following the article, the teens were then asked to read written statements from their older peers reflecting the same message. The final, but most important, step in the process involved the teens writing about how the ideas contained in the article applied to them and their situation. The whole

---

[27] Yeager, D. S., Johnson, R., Spitzer, B. J., Trzesniewski, K. H., Powers, J., & Dweck, C. S. (2014). The far-reaching effects of believing people can change: Implicit theories of personality shape stress, health, and achievement during adolescence. *Journal of Personality and Social Psychology, 106*(6), 867–884. doi:10.1037/a0036335 (freely available here: https://www.researchgate.net/publication/262538735)

process was clear, simple, and as you can see from the results of the study, had a long-lasting effect on all participants.

When looking at changing a person's mindset, even the tiniest mindset interventions work. They change you from the deepest level and have a substantial transformative effect that draws you closer to your values, goals and ultimately, yourself, so you can tackle anything that comes your way!

I have prepared an activity-reinforcing experiment that will help you to implement what you have learnt and consider its real-life applications. This is an extension of this chapter's mindset intervention. Please download the: "2.5 Writing Challenge" worksheet to finish your mindset intervention.

We have now discussed all the background elements of the concept of mindset, and we've shown you examples of people for whom it clearly worked. If you are interested in finding out more, take a look at the research conducted by Associate Professor Greg Walton of Stanford University.[28]

However, I don't want you to challenge only your stress mindset. I would like you to understand, on the deepest level, that all unhelpful beliefs can be challenged – all the 'norms', 'shoulds' , 'ought tos' and 'musts' that bring so much frustration and stress into your life, no matter what they are about. You can challenge them and create more meaningful, balanced beliefs. Try using: "2.6 Should, Ought to, and Must" printable worksheet. By staying balanced, I don't mean donning rose-tinted glasses to even everything out... well, perhaps a

---

[28] Research website of Gregory Walton at Stanford: Walton, G. (2015). Research. Retrieved February 2, 2017, from http://gregorywalton-stanford.weebly.com/research.html

little bit! I mean a dose of healthy, realistic optimism as a basis to your new mindset and emotional resilience, "a person's capacity to cope with changes and challenges, and to bounce back during difficult times."[29]

False and Unrealistic Expectations

Expectations (all those 'shoulds', 'ought tos' and 'musts') that are not based on our own values and abilities are false and unrealistic. False expectations can be our own unrealistic ideas about ourselves and what we believe will happen e.g. I should be able to clean the house top to bottom in two hours. However, they are just as often about external situations/events or other people, e.g. our partner, spouse, work colleagues, or our kids such as: my wife must have packed that; my kids should be more polite; my colleagues ought to do more work.

These expectations are often highly influenced by where we live, the society around us, our culture, the media, family, religion etc. – sometimes to the point that they don't really reflect our own points of view.

However, we need to recognise our internal motivations and set our own standards in accordance with our deepest values and needs. We also need to make specific plans (SMART goals) for living according to those standards that we wish to embody. If we do not create realistic standards for ourselves, we will fail to live up to the false/unrealistic expectations which have come through all the external sources

---

[29] Promoting resilience and wellbeing. (2014). Retrieved February 2, 2017, from www.responseability.org, http://himh.clients.squiz.net/__data/assets/pdf_file/0017/10538/Promoting-Resilience-and-Wellbeing-Final.pdf

mentioned above. This will only bring about a lack of self-esteem, and feelings of disappointment, burnout, anxiety, and depression.

Here are some of the outcomes of living by false (unrealistic) expectations:

- If you expect a lot, and reality does not live up to your expectations, you will feel bad or disappointed.

- If you expect little and the experience is poor, then you were prepared.

- If you expect lots and the experience is great, the anticipation plus the fact will make you feel fantastic!

- If you expect little and the experience is great, it's a fantastic surprise!

However, you can adjust your expectation by mentally preparing yourself for the possible outcomes, either bad or good. Here's a basic example of preparing for a Winter holiday. You are looking forward to it a lot because you love snow and want to relax and enjoy yourself. This is not unrealistic, but what if things don't go to plan? You need to think for a few moments – it doesn't have to be long – about what the possible outcomes could be:

- What could be the **worst** that could happen during your Winter holidays? No snow or heating in the house!

- What could be the **best** scenario? Awesome food, lovely winter conditions, and kids that don't argue.

- What is the **likely** outcome? Possibly a few days without snow.

Can you prepare mentally for each of these situations? What could you do to prepare?

- Investigate non-snow related activities near your accommodation; investigate indoor activities; bring extra thermal layers to wear.

- No need to prepare – everything will be awesome.

- Plan some non-snow related activities (cinema, bowling, board games); bring/ask kids to bring plenty of alternative entertainment.

When we expect too much, we are assuming we have (or should have) control where we might not truly have it. Here are some of the root causes of these unrealistic expectations, and the possible results of living according to them:

- **Setting unrealistic standards (perfectionism)** for self or others can result in never feeling good enough.

- **Criticism of self or others** can result in focusing on mistakes, imperfections, and overlooking the good.

- **People pleasing** can result in trying to be liked by everyone and fitting in with what you think they want, rather than being your amazing, unique self and living congruently to your own, deeply held core values.

- **Doing too much without adequate rest or expecting others to do likewise** can result in burnout and mental or physical illness.

- **Black-and-white thinking** can result in everything seeming either amazing or awful (unrealistic view).

- **Lack of flexibility** can result in arguments, missing out on opportunities/events, boredom and dissatisfaction (especially with kids or partner due to lack of spontaneity).

- **Imbalance between achievements as a source of self-worth and mistakes as failures that are worth more** can result in low self-esteem, disappointment in yourself, and low self-worth.

Some suggested fixes to these could be:

- **Good enough is good enough** – set *realistic* goals (according to your abilities, time, etc. use SMART methodology) and reasonable 'lacking' is allowed; i.e. it doesn't have to be perfect, and if you miss something, it's not the end of the world. Tomorrow is a new day and you get to have another chance to try again.

- **Focus on appreciation of others and your surroundings** – seeing the good every day.

- **Realise the value of your own time and self** – you are a beautiful and unique human being and you only get your time once, so don't waste it living up to other people's standards.

- **Accept ups and downs** – nobody is running at 100% all the time; downtime is an inviolable necessity. Life works on an oscillating pattern; a flat line (using your energy in a linear fashion with no breaks) means you're dead!

- **Practise realistic optimism** – seeing things for what they are (lots of grey) with a positive spin – life is good; nobody is perfect; tomorrow is a new day; you're well off relatively speaking; etc.

Do you know your values and expectations? Take a look at the "2.6 Should, Ought to, and Must" worksheet. You need to know your current abilities, but you must remember that they won't stay the same for the rest of your life. You will learn and grow as a person; you will overcome challenges. These will allow you to gradually push yourself past where you were before, but by continuing to follow realistic expectations.

Choosing Your Mindset(s)

"You live in the story of your life, so you may as well write a good story."
(Maeve)

Fostering flexible optimistic mindsets, kindness, and values

When challenging unhelpful mindsets and beliefs, pay attention to what you wish to replace them with; make a conscious choice that will reflect who you are, who you want to be, and the values that are most important to you. Southwick and Charney studied resilient people for over 20 years and are experts in post-traumatic stress. They studied how truly resilient people bounce back from traumatic situations and stress. These individuals included combat veterans, Special Forces instructors and civilians who had survived major trauma or abuse. They identified realistic optimism, humour, and a strong value system as some of the key elements that could be attributed to boosting emotional resilience and coping skills. They found that realistic optimists suffered less stress and were able to find the will and motivation to withstand difficulty and accomplish their goal when faced with adversity. In general, those who exhibit true resilience are happier than others, and know when to quit and when *not* to quit (and when to laugh). No need to ignore negatives – hence being realistic.

> "... realistic optimists pay close attention to negative information that is relevant to the problems they face. However, unlike pessimists, they do not remain focussed on the negative. They tend to disengage rapidly from problems that appear to be unsolvable. That is, they know when to cut their losses and turn their attention to problems that they believe they can solve." [30]

Here's a quick way to check whether you lean towards pessimism or optimism: think about who you are and how you react to circumstances. If something doesn't go according to plan, you are likely to have engage in one of the following internal dialogues:

> A) "Nothing ever goes the way I want. I can't do anything right. This is all my fault." or;

---

[30] Southwick, S. M. & Charney, D. S. (2012). *Resilience: The Science of Mastering Life's Greatest Challenges.* Cambridge: Cambridge University Press

B) "It's not always this bad. When (something) happens, I will feel better. This wasn't my fault, just an unlucky accident."

If you find yourself consistently turning to B, then count yourself lucky! If you have a tendency towards A, then you may need to pay extra attention to the next few paragraphs about recognising your own **'explanatory style'.**

Explanatory style is the term used to describe how we tend to speak to ourselves and explain why things happen to us. This is highly subjective. In their excellent book, Schwartz and Loehr (2004: 159) discuss Perception and Reality:

"... we deceive ourselves [...] by assuming that our view represents the truth when it is really just an interpretation, a lens through which we choose to view the world. Without realising it, we often create stories around a set of facts and then take our stories to be the truth. Just because something *feels* real to us doesn't make it so. The facts in a given situation may be incontrovertible, but the meaning that we ascribe to them is often far more subjective." [31]

Try to pay attention to the way you talk to yourself when something doesn't go according to plan. What kind of self-talk do you use? How do you explain to yourself why something happened to you? How often do you find yourself thinking, 'This will never end' (it's permanent); 'nobody will ever like me' (universal truth); 'this is all my fault' (it's personal and the world has got it in for me)"? According to

---

[31] Schwartz, T., & Loehr, J. E. (2004). *The Power of Full Engagement: Managing energy, not time, is the key to high performance and personal renewal*. New York: Simon & Schuster Adult Publishing Group.

Martin Seligman,[32] this is a style supporting **'learned helplessness'**. This is your inner pessimist talking based on failure (perceived or real), defeat (perceived or real), and believing that anything you do in the future is futile (definitely unreal). Remember, your mindset must enhance your life, empower you, and help you face your challenges. You are not helpless![33]

With that in mind, how can you foster or grow your capacity for realistic optimism, and snigger in the face of the rubbish called helplessness? Make sure your inner talk (explanatory style) is kind and you treat yourself as you would your best friend – in a loving, honest, and most of all, genuine way. Examples of such self-talk that battles learned helplessness are:

A) I am more than able to handle this situation;

B) This is temporary and short-lived;

C) What happened is unlikely to happen again, and it doesn't relate to my whole experience;

D) This isn't personal, and it isn't all my fault.

---

[32] Seligman, M. E. P. (2006). Learned Optimism: How to Change Your Mind and Your Life. Vintage: New York.

[33] The opposite of "help-less", linguistically, would be "help-full" and that is exactly how you can challenge this situation – you can be helpful to others (see oxytocin and social aspect of life in chapter 4). You might not be able to help your own situation, but being helpful to others will make you feel better. It will build your support network, and who knows what goodness it might bring back into your own situation.

Seligman (2006, ibid) explains: "The defining characteristic of pessimists is that they tend to believe bad events will last a long time, will undermine everything they do and are their own fault" This makes their self-talk permanent, universal, and personal. On the other hand:

"The optimists, who are confronted with the same hard knocks of this world, think about misfortune in the opposite way. They tend to believe defeat is just a temporary setback, that its causes are confined to this one case. The optimists believe defeat is not their fault: Circumstances, bad luck, or other people brought it about. Such people are unfazed by defeat. Confronted by a bad situation, they perceive it as a challenge and try harder."

In our daily lives, it is necessary to take into consideration every piece of negative information presented to us when faced with a challenge. In some jobs, in fact, this is necessary and highly desirable as it helps us to foresee all possible negative outcomes and dangers (lawyers, inspectors, policemen etc.). Sadly, people in those jobs are likely to also suffer from increased stress levels, which lead to both physical and mental health issues. That is, unless they learn to think and cope flexibly – being able to switch their 'inner pessimist' off.

If you are unsure whether to switch your inner pessimist on, ask yourself: Is it meaningful enough to lose my positive mindset, my peace or my optimism? Is it a Code Red type of situation such as:

- Am I, or are others in danger, if I don't think of all the negative eventualities now?

- Are my values or goals going to be destroyed or hampered?

There are plenty of examples:

• Thinking about having a glass of wine or two with friends before driving? Pessimist mode ON! Yes, you would be putting yourself and others in danger. Yes, you **will** get caught. It is *definitely* worth thinking critically in this situation!

• Did you achieve your goal and quit smoking, but you had a tough day at work and feel like having one more cigarette? Pessimist mode ON again. That one cigarette will set you back and could mean it won't be the last one. Will you give up all your progress up to this point for a single hit of dopamine, which you could get from other things such as exercise, chocolate or a hug (not necessarily in that order ☺)?

• Thinking about volunteering or applying for a better job? Pessimist mode OFF! The discomfort you feel before and during an interview is temporary AND you will feel excited (not overly stressed) before and during an interview. Even if you are nervous, it will show people how much the job means to you and being honest and doing your best will only be to your advantage. Even if you don't get the job or volunteering position, you will have had another experience you can use in the future. You would have challenged yourself, grown through, and learned from the experience.

Just as with using stress to your advantage for motivation and energy (and knowing when not to), you also need to learn to turn your inner pessimist on/off. It is crucial to your happiness to be able to recognise and discard an unhelpful coping strategy and replace it with a new, more helpful one. How about switching that chocolate bar for an apple – it's healthier and you will feel more virtuous – also, not spiking your blood sugar levels as dramatically will help with mood regulation.

Know yourself and your values (now and forever)

Your mindset is based on and enhanced by **values** that guide how you live your life, prioritise, and how you make important decisions. Your values tell you who you are and what you stand for. They are your internal satnav when making decisions. They keep you on the straight and narrow; they are there to tell you what you need to do even when your resolve falters.[34] They help you measure yourself to your expectations. They are the basis of your **willpower**.

Here are a few statements that usually get people fired up. They speak tons of values each, depending on whether you agree or disagree. Have a look at them and see what you think (you are not allowed to react 'maybe' or 'depends'!):

- Avoiding paying your fare on the bus or train is ok if they don't catch you;

- It's ok to split the bill on the first date (equality);

- Life in prison should mean no parole, ever;

- Money and ownership is the source of freedom;

---

[34] Barker, E. (2016, April 24). Emotional resilience: How to boost it with 10 research-backed secrets - barking up the wrong tree. Retrieved January 29, 2017, from Become A Great Leader, http://www.bakadesuyo.com/2016/04/emotional-resilience/

- All wars are illegal;

- Self-confidence is learned, not innate;

- I was born poor, so there's no point trying to better myself;

- I didn't do well at school, so I will never achieve a high-paying job;

- I can't quit smoking, because I have failed too many times already;

- Everyone should be paid the same, for the same job, men, women, young workers;

- Gay marriage should be legal everywhere in the world.

Some values can be a bit flexible, some are rigid, and some deepen/strengthen the older we get. Although they are quite stable, significant life changes such as becoming a parent, or experiencing major illness or trauma in your life, can cause your values to shift. Instead of valuing success and financial rewards at work, your focus may shift towards valuing work/life balance and time with your family, friends, or hobbies. With shifting values, the meaning you attribute to your life and what you are passionate about can also shift. An unawareness of the shift in our values can lead to the feeling of lack of direction, meaninglessness and unhappiness.

Therefore, it is very important to identify your core values and regularly keep in touch with what they are. Check out the worksheet: "2.7 Identifying Core Values".

When we don't behave in accordance with our values, it can bring a lot of discontent and unhappiness to our lives. Besides shifting values over time, on many occasions, our values get twisted or bent to fit with our rushed lives. Sometimes, we are so close to the issue that we don't even see our failure to reflect the values that we publicly and privately endorse. This then creates a gap between our inner, value-based being and the reality we are playing out. Our values, or our lack of holding to those we say we believe in, can then become the basis for regrets!

Take, for example, my relationship with my family. I live abroad; my parents aren't together – they have lots of issues (don't we all!) and are not easy to deal with (family!). Although I love them dearly, and know that I want to, and should (watch for how I use it here) be in touch with them more often, I often find myself postponing our conversations because of this and that. It's usually meaningless tasks like washing the dishes, cleaning the kitchen after dinner, checking my phone for messages/emails/bank statements, watching a movie with hubby... that get in the way. I find that I often tell myself off for not getting in touch and leaving it until it's too late in the evening to call anyone. Then the next day, I'll be too busy... etc. It makes me unhappy, yet the solution is simple. But how do you stop your values from being steamrolled into regrets?

> 1) Identify your core value – my core value is 'family care'. Reality and priorities check first. What is most important and more meaningful? Having my house clean before I go to bed or speaking to my parents and having a clean conscience?
>
> 2) Identify the obstacles stopping you from living according to that value and remedy the situation; e.g. If

you didn't have enough time to clean the kitchen in the evening or on the following morning, you could ask for help from your children and partner, or try to clean as you cook.

3) Check your expectations and show a bit of kindness to yourself. It's ok if you can't manage to do something you planned one day – for whatever reason, so just make an unchangeable appointment with yourself for next time – a specific time and date to make sure you do what you need to.

Show a little bit of kindness and compassion to your 'self'!

The reason we need to show ourselves some compassion is the way our brain works. It is very easy to heap guilt and shame on yourself at difficult times, because it activates similar regions in your brain's reward centre. Luckily, it is also a similar reaction to when we feel pride, so we can use that to substitute one feeling for another.

So, we know we can switch the unhelpful thinking for a more helpful habit (you will see more on habits in Chapter 3). Ask yourself in these moments of feeling low, guilty, or ashamed: 'What am I proud of?'. If you know you are often feeling low or anxious and are unlikely to think positively on the spot, make yourself a card and carry it in your purse or wallet for these moments. You can make it a photo or a few of the achievements and best times of your life.

You cannot delete or think away all of your negative experiences, but you would not be the person you are now if you did. So, move on; be proud of what you have achieved; disengage from what you cannot change and trust yourself to do better in the future. Use the strategies for handling negativity in the: "2.8 Challenging Negative Self-Talk" worksheet.

Regrets often show us the values we hold dear, but we only realise them in retrospect when thinking of what we could have done better. So how can we avoid regrets and realise our values ahead of time? Look ahead with your optimistic futurescope. Consider what the **best possible version** of you could be in the future, in comparison with who you are now.

What would your future self tell you to do if they had a chance? What do you think you would regret doing or not doing? Would you regret not asking your colleague out on a date? Not taking that exciting job opportunity abroad? Not quitting smoking? Not doing more exercise? Not spending more quality time with friends or family? Or would you regret telling everyone you were fine when you needed to ask for help? Would you regret not doing enough or doing too little? As crazy as it sounds – or reads, really – it works for me and I really hope it will help you identify your values and what carries real meaning in your life.

You can aspire to be like someone great (e.g. the Dalai Lama, Elon Musk, Steve Jobs, Usain Bolt), but you can only become the best possible version of yourself and that is *something*; that is enough. Use your awesome future self as a role model!

Vision – Translating your Mindset and Values into a Meaningful Life

"I believe each of us has a mission in life, and that one cannot truly be living their most fulfilled life until they

recognize this mission and dedicate their life to pursuing it." [35]
Blake Mycoskie, 2010 (TOMS Shoes founder)

My definition of a vision is 'knowing the direction in which you would like to proceed and the means you are prepared to use to get there'. It encompasses your mindset, values, and who you intend to be. Stress and anxiety are often based on the unknown or the fear of the unknown. However, they are at their worst when you feel you are ill-equipped to cope with your current or future circumstances and when you see your situation as meaningless (whether it be pain, psychological suffering, or day-to-day niggles). By formulating your vision based on who you are, your beliefs and the means by which you are willing get where you want to be, you will introduce the elements of control and meaning into your life. Your vision, and thus knowledge of your direction, will help you feel excited, rather than fearful, about the prospect of what's coming. It will help you rise to the challenge and create a feeling of control and empowerment rather than anxiety and worry.

Think about it as a mission statement for your own life – giving you purpose, a roadmap and knowledge of why your hard work has been worth it. This is a promise you make to yourself; one to focus on when the going gets tough and your journey takes an unexpected turn. Yes, you will still have to deal with frustrating, stressful, or downright traumatic events (visiting in-laws, moving house, quitting a job you don't like – or one that you do). But you won't feel unprepared, and

---

[35] Mycoskie, B. (2010, March 18). Fulfilling my life's mission through the TOMS shoes movement. *Huffington Post*. Retrieved from http://www.huffingtonpost.com/blake-mycoskie/fulfilling-my-lifes-missi_b_362589.html

you will know the true value of whatever stressful situation you find yourself in and why you are going through it. Remember the ACT on stress worksheet, you will be able to A – Acknowledge when you are stressed or anxious and you will understand why you C – Care; why your feelings are meaningful in that moment – and you will learn to T – Transform the anxiety/stress based energy into a meaningful action.

How to formulate and clarify your life's vision

I'm intentionally very specific in saying that vision is close, but not equal to, a dream. In my mind, a dream is something you can aspire to, but is often unattainable in the future. It is based on your imagination of who you are and what you would like to achieve, and generally disregards the reality, resources, and the amount of hard work you will need to put in. I'm not saying don't dream, or don't dream big – dreaming is the backbone of creativity and future innovation; but without a reality check followed by action, dreams are just dreams.

Vision, on the other hand, is firmly based on realistic expectations, possibilities, your mindset and values; it's based on really knowing yourself. It is purposeful, optimistic but achievable, meaningful, and fulfilling to *you* and your future self! Yet how do you formulate your vision and how do you know what is truly important to you? There are a few indicators you can think of when considering what it is that gives your life meaning and brings out the best in you. Look at your current regrets (remember those are your values that have been squashed and bashed): what you are proud of in your future self, role model, or superhero and what do you want your friends to remember you by when you die?

Considering your vision

Hint #1 Regrets:

What are your regrets? Or what would you most regret if you were to die tomorrow? Well, I did not say this will be easy! This is a bit on the heavy side, but sometimes a hard shove in the right direction is what is needed to move forward.

Although it is fashionable nowadays to say, "I don't regret anything I have done," keep in mind that you are more likely to regret something you haven't done than something you have done or do regularly (about 75/25 ratio).[36] If you can't think of any regrets, Bronnie Ware[37] has collated some in a heartfelt memoir of her work in palliative care. She found that the most frequent regrets were:

1) I wish I'd had the courage to live a life true to myself, not the life others expected of me;

2) I wish I hadn't worked so hard;

3) I wish I'd had the courage to express my feelings;

4) I wish I'd stayed in touch with my friends;

5) I wish that I had let myself be happier.

---

[36] Morrison, M., & Roese, N. J. (2011). Regrets of the typical American. Social Psychological and Personality Science, 2(6), 576–583. doi:10.1177/1948550611401756

[37] Ware, B. (2012). The top five regrets of the dying: A life transformed by the dearly departing. Carlsbad, CA: Hay House.

I'm sure you will come up with some as well. Amongst mine were: I wish I had exercised more; I wish I had changed my job and prioritised my health; I wish I had kept up my language skills in German and French; I wish I'd kept in touch with my friends; I wish I was better at communicating with my family; I wish I had volunteered as soon as that thought crossed my mind the first time. I could go on and on...

When you have a list, look at it closely. What values do they speak of? Care for one's wellbeing? Purpose and meaning instead of financial reward? Social connection? Which ones are optimistic, empowering, healthy, and just right for you? You may find the: "2.9 Regret, Value, Next Step" worksheet helpful.

Hint #2 What do I love about my future self, role-model, or a favourite superhero?

When you look in your futurescope, what values and life's vision or path did your future amazing self follow? What are you good at now but amazing at in the future? Do you like spotting errors in the newspapers or in work documentation? Did your future self build themselves a proofreading business or a funny blog? Do you also give some of your time to a charity, helping to check their website and printed documents for any errors? Yours may be very different to my list here. If you find it hard imagining a successful self in the future, think, 'What am I good at now but could be amazing at in the future?' Another good question to ask is: what are the qualities I identify with in my superhero or role model? Is it perseverance, trying new things, being brave and courageous, and taking (calculated) risks? Or is it taking the plunge and becoming a stay-at-home parent, and following your heart?

Hint #3 Your eulogy

Richard Wiseman (2010)[38] suggests to imagine your friends and family talking at your funeral, giving a eulogy on your achievements and legacy. Are you proud of what they are saying? Does it make you feel fulfilled? What is it you want them to remember you for?

Now, you can be as broad or as narrow in your vision as you like. You can settle on a single broad sentence:

> *"My mission in life is not merely to survive, but to thrive; and to do so with some passion, some compassion, some humor, and some style."*[39]
> Maya Angelou, 2017 (American poet)

Alternatively, as Benjamin Franklin did, you can settle on a list of virtues or values to guide your life every day. These are the characteristics or items in your life that you wish to cultivate – and you want to do that every day to keep in touch with yourself, your needs and your values.

My list – for your inspiration:

- Be accepting of change and challenge;

- Foster good work-life balance;

---

[38] Wiseman, R. (2010). *59 seconds: Change your life in under a minute*. New York: Knopf Doubleday Publishing Group.

[39] Angelou, M. (2017, January 27). A quote by maya Angelou. Retrieved January 29, 2017, from http://www.goodreads.com/quotes/11877-my-mission-in-life-is-not-merely-to-survive-but

- Be a good role model for my children and teach them kindness and perseverance;

- Help others and share with others what I have learned;

- Get up if you fall;

- Relax often and laugh every day, even if it is at yourself;

- Embrace silliness and a fresh look at the world as if every day were new (because it is!);

- Do things I want to do, not only things I need to do.

There is no magic formula; there are no magic numbers; 3 or 13 don't matter; it is the quality and follow-up that counts. You can display your list or statement to yourself (and others) proudly as a reminder of who you intend to be and what you need to work on every day. You can even create a credit-card-sized version for your purse or wallet, so you can take these prompts with you everywhere. You could also create a chart to hang inside your wardrobe door to see (more on review shortly) at the beginning and end of your day.

You can do this for yourself, but if you have a family, I would recommend considering doing this exercise as a family (in child-friendly form), to come up and agree on your family's vision. Doing this will help you build values into your family life, and in turn, make your family happier and stronger together. Involving children in this type of decision empowers them. It helps them remember what it means to belong; to be part of your family and reminds them of what you're working towards. This could be respecting personal space, saying please and thank you, going on holidays without stressing about packing, always learning; or it could simply be spending time together and having fun regularly (e.g. watch a film together every Friday).[40]

Make sure, regardless of what you choose for your vision or mission in life, that it is true to yourself and not to the expectations of others. If you want to be happier, less stressed and anxious, and pursue a more meaningful life, you need to start with yourself first.

How to Pursue Your Life's Vision

"It's not enough to be busy, so are the ants. The question is, what are we busy about?" [41]
Henry David Thoreau (1817 – 1862)

Set goals

It would be safe to assume that your life's vision is a grand one, but how you go about getting there is a different issue altogether. Whether you have one master vision or a set of virtues to work on throughout your life, you will need to make it manageable and achievable by breaking it into smaller chunks that can easily be managed along the way. You will need to look at setting intermediate and short-term goals or strategies to help you achieve and practise being who you intend to be.

Engaging in **planning** small, achievable goals will not only help your stress levels, but it will also increase your self-confidence and help

---

[40] Feiler, B. (2013). The Secrets of Happy Families: Improve your mornings, tell your family history, fight smarter, go out and play, and much more. New York: HarperCollins.

[41] Thoreau, H. D. (2016, January 13). A quote by Henry David Thoreau. Retrieved January 29, 2017, from http://www.goodreads.com/quotes/7273089-it-s-not-enough-to-be-busy-so-are-the-ants

with motivation as you see yourself progressing towards your main goal. Your brain will be rewarded by the pleasure-related hormone, dopamine, every time you achieve a goal, reinforcing the motivation to progress and reward yourself again. You can even make the journey more pleasant by setting a lot of smaller goals – the more the merrier, and the more dopamine you will enjoy!

When setting any goals for yourself, you should always use these questions as a guide:

- Is it realistic?

- Is it in line with my vision?

- Is it helping me achieve my ultimate vision?

- Does it teach me anything?

- Does it empower me?

Look at each day as a new opportunity to take gracious pride in whatever you happen to be doing in that moment. Give yourself credit for every daily success. Determine your priorities, and be mindful in accomplishing them.

Review and track your progress – be flexible

We've already touched briefly on the importance of reviewing your values and vision, but in order to make sure that the progress you are making toward your goals is in alignment with your vision and values, you must review and track your progress frequently – even daily. It doesn't matter whether this is with the help of a diary, star chart or an app such as Wunderlist, or through writing a blog for others to read.

However, be aware that accountability rarely comes from the outside (unlike support). You need to hold yourself accountable for staying on track – nobody else will do that for you. You can share your vision with others and hope that others may help you keep an eye on the 'prize', but they can't make you follow your own vision. Others can provide mental and practical support as well as much needed feedback. However, you need to (what I like to call) 'parent yourself' and take responsibility for your own actions. Support in yourself those behaviours and strategies that you would like to develop in your offspring. Learn from what you did or didn't do, and what worked or didn't.

You also need to be aware that as you move from one stage of life to another, what gives it meaning might shift and your dreams might change. If you don't check in with your values and yourself often, you may realise that you were so busy trying to get to your goal that you didn't notice your dreams changing in the meantime. The things that you once thought were important no longer matter to you; or perhaps you got side-tracked and are heading elsewhere. You need to cultivate awareness of the big picture as well as the small and big life events; be mindful of their value and impact, and be **flexible** enough to realise that you or your dreams can change.

One great strategy for creating and reviewing your goals is to use the SMART goals methodology. SMART stands for:

- **S**pecific (Is my goal direct and to the point?);

- **M**easurable (How will I know that I have achieved my goal?);

- **A**chievable (What strategies will I use to achieve my goal?);

LEARN TO LOVE STRESS

- **R**ealistic (Is this the next logical step in my progress?);

- **T**ime-bound (When will I 'check in' to see if my goal has been achieved?)

Applying these five principles to each goal can help you to clarify, track, and attain your goal in a realistic manner and in a realistic timeframe, according to your own resources, whether these are physical, mental, financial, spatial, or something else. There are variations of the SMART methodology that add further letters or use slightly different meanings for each of the letters, but the core principle is the same. Any version of the SMART goal methodology can be used as a tool for avoiding outlandish goal-setting. This does not mean that you can't shoot for the stars, though! If you have a big, bold dream, e.g. 'put man on Mars', then you just need to apply the SMART acronym to your goal:

- Specific – Mankind will travel to Mars (i.e. it must be a human, not dogs, insects, etc.);

- Measurable – How will I know it has been achieved? (A human being will be observed setting foot on Mars.);

- Achievable – What strategy will I use to make this happen? (Which technology will be needed? Do I need to use certain people or resources?)

- Realistic – Is this the next logical step? (Man has already landed on the Moon, so Mars next is a logical progression.)

- Time-bound – When will I check to see if I have achieved the goal? (Set a timeframe and work towards achieving your goal within it).

Commit, prepare to fail, and persevere

"When we lack a strong sense of purpose we are easily buffeted by life's inevitable storms."
(Schwartz and Loehr, 2004:146)

Of course, not everything always goes to plan; your new Mars rocket might explode upon take-off. It's important to remember that life is amazing and a great gift, but it can also be difficult, and an immense challenge at times. It is inevitable that in life you will find yourself in all kinds of circumstances due to health issues, decisions you make, and elements that are completely beyond your control.

Luckily, you don't need to be the smartest, fastest or most daring to follow your vision and succeed. What brings about success is commitment, perseverance and acceptance of the reality that sometimes you will fail. If you're reading this book and you've gotten this far, then you understand that now is the moment for you to start making a **commitment to yourself and your values for change**. You need to acknowledge that it will be hard work and that you will need to persevere both through and despite challenges. Most importantly, if you do nothing, nothing will change. Some days, you will follow your vision and achieve your goals and other days, for whatever reason, you won't be able to achieve what you set out to do that day.

Failure happens no matter how much you worry about an outcome or how good your intentions are. It is a natural part of life. As Denis Waitley (1984) [42] said:

---

[42] Waitley, D. (1984). *Seeds of greatness: The ten best-kept secrets of total success.* New York: Simon & Schuster.

"Failure should be our teacher, not our undertaker. Failure is delay, not defeat. It is a temporary detour, not a dead end. Failure is something we can avoid only by saying nothing, doing nothing, and being nothing".

There is no need to fear failure, as it only leads to defeat if we can't learn from it. Reviewing and being able to look at your failure is the first step to learning and succeeding next time. Sometimes, things will not go the way you want them to; you may or may not be able to influence how things pan out, but you can affect the way you react and what you do next – and that is what counts. So, don't give up! You only fail if you give up, or fail to learn from the setbacks you experience.

It can be difficult not to lose sight of who you are and to keep on track with what you wish to achieve when dealing with stress and anxiety. In the following chapter, we will show you more strategies and ways of keeping your sight on what is meaningful to you and how to achieve your ambitions; while making your life a whole lot happier and the journey whole lot more enjoyable.

Don't be discouraged by a winding path to success. It still is a path to success, but it is also a promise to take you along the scenic route, with lots of meaningful moments – and some fun along the way! The secret is learning to laugh at yourself.

Just to re-cap: How do you strike a balanced mindset between being an awesome, all-perceiving pessimistic lawyer prone to heart disease and divorce, and a happy healthy bunny in rose-tinted glasses?

A) ACT on stress and anxiety.

B) Challenge negative thinking and practise realistic optimism. (Hard work – consider yourself forewarned!)

C) Find your pessimism on/off switch and use it cautiously and sparingly.

D) Know yourself and your values – formulate a vision (mission statement of your life).

D) Keep an eye on your vision and with every goal, ask yourself: Is it realistic, Is it in line with my vision? Is it helping me achieve my ultimate vision/goal? Does it teach me anything/ Does it empower me? Use SMART methodology or another strategy that suits you best.

E) Commit and persevere through challenges – there will be plenty.

F) Plan for the eventualities you can control and to which you can make a difference; and let go of those that are unsolvable.

Summary of Chapter 2

• Your mindsets are guided by your beliefs, and you can change them.

• Embracing your inner optimist relieves the negative effects of stress.

• Knowing yourself and your values helps you meet challenges with more willpower.

• Formulating a vision for your life will give you direction.

• Track your progress and review regularly – this helps you to keep going.

• You can learn to be flexible – it's in your nature as a human being to adapt.

• Failure is part of trying; it is a learning opportunity.

Chapter 3: The Structure of Your Life and Maintaining Change

<u>Keywords for this chapter:</u>
Bullet-proofing
Emotional resilience
Taking control
Rituals, routines, and habits
Time and energy management and prioritisation

Maintaining change in mentality isn't easy and it takes time for this way of thinking, or any for that matter, to become automatic. However, there are many ways in which we can help (one might say trick) our brain into accepting and automating these processes quicker, and with more ease. We can do this by:

- freeing our mind's resources by creating helpful coping habits, routines, and rituals;

- bullet-proofing our life by planning, and increasing emotional resilience.

Bullet-Proofing my Life and Building Emotional Resilience – Where do I Start?!

I've talked about how your mindset can greatly influence both your physical and psychological responses to stressful or anxiety-inducing moments. You'll have read how you can use 'stress' to your advantage through simple, yet effective interventions. I have mentioned the importance of nurturing your inner realistic optimist; and how formulating a meaningful vision can change your life and help you stay motivated and on-track towards a happier and more positive life. Remember, that it is the pursuit of meaning in your life that empowers you and gives you strength to cope with stress in a positive way.

Considering setbacks

However, we know that there are things in our lives – some avoidable and some not, that can distract us, get in our way or just plain stop us from achieving what we set out to do and how we set out to live. This could be anything from feeling low and tired in the morning and lacking motivation, to being discouraged by people we meet. Or you could be encountering medical issues or experience car breakdown on the way to work. I'm sure you could come up with tonnes of examples from your own life. Honestly, it can feel like you're being hammered by shots out of nowhere.

If a setback hits you, it is more likely that you will revert to your old habits of thinking and behaviour, stress and anxiety responses. This is why planning and resilience strategies need to go hand-in-hand to make you and your life bulletproof. It doesn't mean that you won't be hit by anything; setbacks, bad news, and even friendly fire are all part of life, especially if you're doing something right! However, people who wear bulletproof vests know that there is a chance they will get hit and it will hurt, but they will survive and keep doing what they believe in. So, we learn from them. We plan for unfavourable eventualities, but still vigorously pursue what we believe in.

Part of bullet-proofing your life and building emotional resilience is considering your coping habits. Are they helpful or not? Good, or bad? Do they help you achieve your life's vision, and help you live an empowered and emotionally resilient life? Do they help you cope with everyday challenges, as well as bounce back from major setbacks? Or, are your coping habits helping you slip down a narrow spiral of avoidance, isolation and conscious (or subconscious) self-harm and disempowerment?

Take smoking for example. You say 'I'm gonna quit,' but then you get stressed and anxious about life, or even about what you're going to feel like when you don't have a cig for a whole day... So you light up again to chill out! It feels good at the time, but it pushes the goal – quitting smoking – further away, and so most people end up feeling resentful towards themselves. You feel like a failure and then that makes you way more likely to give up on the goal altogether. Obviously, this is an unhelpful coping habit, but before you change it, you need to be aware of what is actually happening and how habits work. Whether consciously or subconsciously, habits have a massive impact on your everyday life, and whether, as well as how you reach your goals. The good news is that there are relatively easy ways of establishing good habits, routines, rituals and practices in our lives that will help us become happier, less anxious, and more productive and resilient. The reality is that it does take some time, patience and commitment for this to work.

I will go through the steps you need to establish good practices in your life and give you the tools to help you keep them. I want to help you integrate good things into your life; to help you achieve your goals, and become a more practical, productive and happier self. You truly can become more like those athletes we mentioned in the first chapter. You can learn to thrive on stress and turn anxious feelings to better use, instead of being a slave to them.

Taking Control

You have probably heard the phrase 'life is a journey'. So, I'd like to start by using the analogy of a long road trip...

You are the driver. You are responsible for the safety of yourself, the car, and any passengers who might be travelling with you. You are not just driving around randomly, in circles; you are following a road. You're attempting to get to a destination on the other side of the country. It's a long trip, so you need to be prepared for it. Just like with our bodies, the basics need to be taken care of first, i.e. the car's 'health'. It needs to be roadworthy. It needs regular fuel; it can't go on driving forever; and it needs to be cleaned – just like us. We need food, rest, and a wash. If you don't get these basics sorted, there is only so long a journey will last before something terrible happens and you wind up broken down, dead, or seriously injured. Along the way, you'll come across amazing sights, meet some awesome people, and have a lot of fun. You'll also encounter obstacles, run out of fuel, maybe break down, and probably make a few wrong turns. But it's OK! It's all part of the journey, and you can always start again where you last left off.

Coping habits

Being in control of your life is about these basic, everyday essentials that help you get to where you're going. Once you establish the basics, they'll just become automatic, almost mechanical. You won't even need to think about them, because you'll do them naturally. Just like when the car is running low on fuel and you pull in and fill up the tank; likewise, when you're hungry, you fuel up your body. But you've got to put the right fuel in. Putting diesel in a petrol tank is not going to make the car work that well... And so it is with us; we need to eat decent food, the right food, and drink plenty of water, or else we'll just stop working properly, or maybe stop forever. Establishing good habits is something most of us were lucky enough to be taught by our parents such as brushing our teeth, eating our veg etc. However, as we grow into adults, the cares of the world often overtake us and we turn to certain things to help us cope. We generally call these 'coping habits'. However, you could even call them 'coping strategies' as that is exactly what they are – a devised plan of action which will empower you at times of challenge.

Avoidance, distraction and denial. These are the three things that some coping habits make us do. They are not strategies, because we have not consciously devised them. They are automatic and unhelpful. They're what we're really fighting against. 'Life is hard! I hate this situation. OK, I'll just avoid it then! I know – I'll just go and play some XBox. It's sitting right in front of me; it's calling my name. I know I've got an exam tomorrow and should be getting a good night's sleep, but this will help me relax – honest.' We deny the reality of our lives because we're afraid. Often, we are afraid of pain and discomfort; afraid of feeling vulnerable. It's OK, though. We all do this, at least at some point in our lives. The problem is when we religiously run away from anything even slightly difficult or uncomfortable. Facing the issue puts us out there and helps us learn and grow. Avoidance reinforces fear and feelings of weakness and vulnerability. But you know what? We're all on our own journey; our own road trip. You need to decide which challenge is worth it (according to your values) and then face the obstacles it brings. By facing challenges and our fears, we can help ourselves, and each other carry on with our journeys. Being prepared to face challenges is a good practice.

Can you think of any habits that help you cope with day-to-day life? Are there any that you don't even think of that you use every day or when the proverbial hits the fan? If you want to respond to stressful situations with a 'this-is-an-awesome-challenge' attitude and a growth mindset, you need to keep your values at the forefront of your thoughts, acknowledge the habits in which you are engaging, and examine their helpfulness. Are these habits or strategies supporting the core values that you want to embody in your life?

There are many situations in our lives that can lead to stress or anxiety. One that often comes up as having a significant impact is job security. It can make you worried about how you will cope both personally and financially, as well as socially, since the job often comes with a social circle and support associated with that. If you lost your job, then the way you felt and what you did immediately afterwards would be largely down to your coping habits, emotions, and the meaning you assigned to what happened. Take a moment to consider how you would feel and what you would do if you suddenly lost your job:

> A. You could be devastated, thinking that you loved the job and were great at it; you might wonder how you will ever find such an interesting, easy, or well-paid job. You could feel that you've done an amazing job that wasn't appreciated, and that could lead to a lot of negative feelings, as well as worries about the future, such as: 'I did my best but I still got sacked; I'm not good at anything. Nobody will ever employ me. I will never find such a great job.'

> B. You could choose to think that a 'change of job' is part of life and nothing stays constant forever. If you hated the job anyway and wanted to leave, then you might be relieved and immediately start looking at what possible better options you have. Even if you feel a little bit of trepidation at the prospect of interviews or financial implications, you might just take this as a good thing, the

necessary impetus to get you moving to a job you like, or one that you always wanted.

The ways in which you usually deal with setbacks, your coping habits, will most likely now present themselves after your initial reaction of A or B. Your coping habits could be unhelpful, consisting of avoidance and distraction e.g. cigarettes, alcohol, food, television or video games. Your other options are helpful coping strategies such as turning to your friends and family for assistance; going for a jog to get your blood pumping and endorphins flowing; or perhaps deciding to put some ideas on paper to create a plan... There are many ways to cope with life and being aware of which habits we employ for coping is extremely important to be able to transform any unhelpful ones to our advantage.

How habits work and how they can be changed

All our lives, we learn to cope with various situations and our brain learns from these. Sometimes this happens extremely quickly — learning that you should wait for a hot cake to cool down before stuffing it in your mouth (you usually only do that once!). Sometimes slowly, hanging your keys onto a key hook where you'll always find them. It might take a while and a few desperate searches to learn that! Your reward is either not hurting yourself and getting a sugar hit from a cool cake or knowing where you left your things. Our brain attaches meaning to everything we do and releases dopamine after a pleasurable action (sugar hit or finding your keys on time). But, curiously, next time we do the same, the dopamine comes earlier and earlier until just thinking about the action releases a dose of dopamine in our brain, thus making us happier. This creates a neural pathway that makes it easier to repeat the same action in the same situation next time.

This is how tasks are automated and habits are born. This is great in a situation when you automatically make a cup of tea without burning yourself. It is not so great when you have trained yourself to automatically turn on the TV instead of exercising or studying. Naturally, we avoid difficult actions, tasks and jobs and replace them with easy or pleasurable things. These could be anything from procrastination (e.g. watching TV instead of studying); eating sugary snacks instead of preparing healthy ones; buying unnecessary things instead of saving up for your dream (new kitchen, holidays, gym membership, going out with friends); or staying at home on your own instead of trying to go out and see your friends.

In situations like these, our amazing brains work against us and subconsciously choose the action that will most likely and most speedily produce the coveted dopamine delivery. I admit that I feel happier eating chocolate with a friend than I do writing an essay, but then I become stressed that my essay has not written itself yet and I have a bit more chocolate to feel better. What the brain does is choose, subconsciously, any coping habit that will make it feel better. Anything that worked in the past and that will release a bit of dopamine quickly – even if it is only temporary and is followed by regret. Dopamine is the shady figure behind your motivation, or lack of it. The more you allow your brain to keep rewarding itself for not doing the things you know are good, necessary or healthy, the less motivation you will have to do the right things.

Surprisingly, almost half of our day is spent living on auto-pilot and following subconscious habits. A 2010 study found not only that people were often living in their heads, on autopilot and with their minds wandering, but they also were unhappy while doing so.[43] We don't even notice that we let our subconscious brain take over and do whatever it pleases. Unfortunately, especially when we are stressed or anxious, what it pleases to do is rarely good for us. Often, it's the easiest and quickest, least productive way to get a dopamine hit. Since it's so frequent, I will say it again. Your subconscious *is in charge almost 50% of your day*! Wouldn't it be nice if we could make this auto-pilot work for us, motivating us towards helpful habits and coping mechanisms? Could we, as a bonus, learn to be happier through living in the moment?

Let's do this, and learn a bit more about the background of our habits and how they work. Your brain is a fantastic machine. That is why it is so efficient at getting that dopamine hit. But we want to train ourselves to have good habits and then get the dopamine reward. There are three main areas of your brain that have a lot to do with habits and how you lead your life, and it's important that you realise how they work both with and against each other to rewire your brain for the better.

> 1) Firstly, you have the bespectacled and studious teacher's pet, your **prefrontal cortex**. It is the rational one – the one that likes planning, intentional action, and going after your goals. It really cares about you, but only while it pays attention;
>
> 2) When it stops paying attention, consciousness slips into sub-conscious decisions and the second one, the **dorsal striatum** (or just **striatum** for short) takes over.

---

[43] Killingsworth, M. A., Gilbert, D. T. (2010). A wandering mind is an unhappy mind. *Brevia*, *330*(6006), 932. doi:10.1126/science.1192439

This is an ancient one, pretending to limp along with a stick, which only wants to do what has been done before. It likes things the way they are and does not like change. It isn't conscious and even though it is ancient and a bit arthritic, as soon as your prefrontal cortex is offline, it acts super fast and slinks down the well-trodden path before you know it. This path could be a neural pathway towards a helpful or unhelpful habit;

3) The third one is your party animal, the **nucleus accumbens**, which only really cares about having fun and doing things that are known to be pleasurable. Be it a tub of Ben & Jerry's ice-cream or cycling, it doesn't matter. If your habit is usually to go for a tub of ice-cream without a bowl your striatum says: 'That's the way it's always been done; so be it,' and the nucleus accumbens will think: 'Hmm… That has always been nice – sugar, dopamine… Pure bliss. Yes, please!'

If you're not ready to fight the corner of your prefrontal cortex on the spot, and stop the other two in their tracks, your good intentions and plans will be outvoted. The nucleus accumbens will enjoy the bliss, the striatum will get its way, and nothing will change. This is fine if you are using a helpful coping habit subconsciously; for example, talking to your friends if you're feeling anxious or going for a run when feeling stressed. It's not so good if your habits lead you to smoking, distractions or isolation.

However, I did say **you can rewire your brain** and teach your striatum new tricks. To do this, you will need to engage your prefrontal cortex more. This can be done through:

1) making plans;

2) following them through;

3) rewarding yourself;

4) making decisions rather than acting subconsciously; and

5) labelling your emotions (remember you can use my worksheet for this) as you go through your day.[44]

Repeating these as often as possible will create new neural pathways. Luckily, the more you plan and follow your plan, the more engaged your prefrontal cortex will be, and this, in turn, will increase your willpower and motivation. If you achieve your goal, even if it's a tiny micro-ambition, your body will release dopamine. This rewards your action, creating a new neural pathway for your striatum, as well as teaching your nucleus accumbens that this new habit is also fun.

The more often you repeat the same action, followed by a reward, the more likely you are to repeat it and create a new more helpful habit that the striatum will subconsciously choose next time. Also, the more often you repeat the same action, the quicker you get the dopamine hit, which in time will precede your action. Imagine you go running every morning (yawn) for two or three months, even just thinking about it will get your brain releasing dopamine to motivate you to do it. How cool is that?!

---

[44] Korb, A. (2015). *The upward spiral: Using Neuroscience to reverse the course of depression, One small change at a time*. United States: New Harbinger Publications.

How long does it take to create new habits or break old ones?

This change will not happen overnight. There are a few extreme cases, such as when smokers become violently sick after inhaling cigarette smoke, or heavy drinkers who suddenly can't stand the smell of booze – but these are *very* rare. Pop culture stands by 'about a month' to make or break a habit, most likely due to a 1960's theory by Maxwell Maltz. However, more recent research done in 2009 by researchers at University College London (UCL)[45] showed that it takes between 18 and 245 days, but on average, it would take 66 days to create a new habit. So there is no reason to despair if you get to the end of the month and you realise that you need to take a few more weeks to make your new behaviour as automatic as the old one. In fact, you should expect it. Unrealistic expectations are the killer of good strategies and habits.

Habits are hard to change! They are meant to be that way. They exist so that our brain frees up resources for dealing with matters that are more pressing than those that we handle every day. Those everyday things can be handled on auto-pilot – you don't need your whole mental acuity to tie your shoelaces or make tea. This is great news for us, as once you establish a good habit like going for a jog every morning, preparing a healthy lunch the night before going to work, or telling yourself you are excited before a speech (instead of anxious), you will not need to exert much self-control to do it on autopilot. Your striatum will do the work for you subconsciously, and the nucleus

---

[45] Lally, P., van Jaarsveld, C. H. M., Potts, H. W. W., & Wardle, J. (2009). How are habits formed: Modelling habit formation in the real world. *European Journal of Social Psychology*, *40*(6), 998–1009. doi:10.1002/ejsp.674

accumbens, as well as the prefrontal cortex, will be happy (dopamine – check; doing something for your wellbeing – check)!

The study from UCL also showed that even if you miss a day here or there where you aren't able to nurture and use your great new habit, you're not a failure and you're not sent back to square one. It is only a myth that all is lost if you miss a day of behaving according to your plan or new habit. Only if you believe this myth will it prevent you from getting back on track and restarting where you left off. We know that our brain stores many actions in our memory, and all we need to do to revive those memories is get back to them and build on them again. However, in order to progress quickly, it is best to be really diligent at least in the first few weeks of starting a new behaviour.

Choosing and introducing a new habit

So how can you break, or get rid of, an unhelpful habit? Well, you don't! Habits don't just disappear; they get replaced by something that is similar, or more pleasurable.[46] It is easier to replace a habit rather than get rid of it completely, which is why chewing gum or tablets works better for quitting smoking than just nicotine patches. This works best if the **Golden Rule of habit change** (Duhigg, 2012 ibid.) is applied, keeping the cue and reward the same, but changing your routine. So, in relation to the smoking example, the cue that starts off the habit is the same (stress, social situation, boredom), but the action is replaced (chewing gum, tablets) and the reward stays the same (nicotine from a different source). Then later, one can work on decreasing nicotine intake and moving onto a healthier gum over time.

[46] Duhigg, C. (2012). *The power of habit: Why we do what we do in life and business*. New York: Random House Publishing Group.

The neural pathway that originally allowed a person to subconsciously reach for a cigarette doesn't just go away – it stays put. Yet, it can become less dominant if you create a new pathway (such as reaching for a gum, or knitting), which is then used and reinforced more frequently and therefore becomes more dominant. It will become your new subconscious port of call – the better-trodden path. The more it is used, the more automatic it will be, slowly shifting the old habit out of the view.

When you're trying to introduce a new habit, hopefully a more helpful one, you need to consider what need your old habit is answering. Is it a need for comfort, relaxation, a dopamine or mood boost, good health, socialising, or feeling included? I watch a lot of television in the evenings with my husband, who says it helps him wind down and feel sleepy. It doesn't work for me the same way, as often, I feel it rather wakes me up and gets me over-excited. Yet, I still sit with him and watch random programmes because I want to spend time with him, but then get annoyed with myself (and him – poor guy!) when I can't fall asleep.

I always thought that a better habit would be to go for a run in the evening. I tried really hard to keep it up, but no matter how healthy it is, and how great I felt afterwards, it didn't work. Now I know why – it's because it simply didn't answer my need for feeling close to and spending time with my husband; which is why I had to rethink replacing the TV watching marathon. I needed to find something that would answer the needs of both of us, i.e. bring us closer, allow us to spend quality time together, and help us both wind down before bed. So, with the support from my hubby, we have created an evening routine where we read our favourite book together aloud. We take turns, laugh at the same jokes, or talk about points that interest us or those that don't make sense. It has become a ritual that we both enjoy very much and that brings us closer together. The bonus point of all this is that since you can't possibly read aloud for two solid hours, we tend to get tired and sleepy before our usual way-too-late-to-go-to-bed time, therefore falling asleep earlier and getting more rest, which makes getting up in the morning with a smile on your face (and dealing with a stroppy toddler or a vile teenager) much easier.

It is important to realise that changing your whole life all at once will be extremely hard. So, start small. I know that after reading the first two chapters you are now geared towards massive change in your life and you want to do it all! But we are not trying to make life difficult and miserable. Rather than splitting your attention between several areas you're trying to tackle, choose one and give it a month or two of undivided attention. Once you know that your new habit is safely in place, add a new one on top of that. If the behaviour that you're trying to nurture is, for example, challenging your negative thinking, make time each day to reflect on your thought patterns and write new, more helpful ones every time. At the end of the month, you will see whether it is now your natural state of mind or whether you need to continue practising for a few more weeks or months to change your thought patterns for the better.

When you find yourself at the stage of using the strategy subconsciously, or at least comfortably throughout the day, consider adding another helpful habit. You will find, however, that challenging negative thinking will bring on other changes naturally, with a big impact throughout your life. These could be an increase in confidence and feeling more sociable because you will be more realistic about what people think of you (not everybody dislikes you). You will become more open to trying new things (yes, you *can*, if you *try*). You will become less anxious as you learn that things are usually not as bad as they seem. This snowballing effect is what you're aiming at with your first change.

The biggest impact is possible through the smallest change. Habits that automatically affect many areas of your life are called **keystone habits** and they have the potential to change how you see yourself (Duhigg, 2012 ibid.). Their effects snowball just like a mindset intervention, bringing on other changes that have a significant impact on your life. Many people take up exercise to become fitter or slimmer. However, it can also result in healthier eating and therefore better health; more endorphins and therefore better moods; exposure to the physical signs of stress and therefore increased stress resilience; and better confidence in your physical ability as well as willpower and sense of achievement which in turn improves social interactions. For some people, this particular keystone habit of exercise can be an avalanche of positive change. "But," I hear you say, "some people are exercising regularly and still suffer from stress and anxiety." Well, in this case, or if you simply don't enjoy exercise in a traditional sense, you can build a swift walk or long leisurely stroll with your loved one into your everyday life; go dancing (or dance in the shower), cycle to work or learn to see cleaning as an exercise. If neither are a good option, you might need to consider other keystone habits such as joining an interest group, taking a course, or using public transport instead of a car.

Keystone habits can be anything that will make you change how you see yourself. How about looking at your future self again, or at your role models. What do they do that is so awesome and make you aspire to something bigger? Do they consciously build and maintain a strong social network (the glue that holds a group of friends together)? Do they volunteer for local groups (generous benefactors and helpers)? Do they keep a journal of positive thoughts and creative ideas (the creative optimist)? Or do they get up early on Saturdays to have time for themselves (self-care and relaxation) so that they are all set and 'zen' for a weekend with their family (taking care of themselves helps them care for their family)? How about learning a new language and going to conversation classes (meeting new people, increasing confidence, able to travel and meet the locals). As you can see, these types of activities can all unlock further benefits and improve your life in a meaningful way.

A plan for building helpful habits into your life

How do you introduce and keep up more helpful coping habits for handling stressful or anxiety-inducing situations, and for that matter all rituals and routines you'd like to stick with?

> 1) You look at yourself and your actions, considering what your needs are, and which unhelpful habits are currently in place to "help you" (e.g. I'm supposed to write 500+ words a day, but before I start I need to check FB/Twitter/etc. so that I keep in touch with friends).

> 2) Then look at keystone habits – anything that'll make you see yourself differently – and choose the one that answers your need (e.g. I want to be in touch with my friends, so maintaining a strong social network outside my writing time would be best).

> 3) Optional – in the case of difficult habits such as smoking – just by counting how many cigarettes you smoke every day over time helps decrease the amount and make you more aware of when you are lighting up subconsciously. In the case of my procrastination and

checking social media, I need to keep a record for a few days of how much time I spend on social media and use this time to actually agree to meet my friends rather than read about them.

4) Make a detailed plan or a checklist and stick with it – put it somewhere very visible in your house, in your calendar or your phone and use an alarm to remind yourself! (whiteboard next to the fridge or on the wardrobe door; phone reminders are also useful).

5) Motivate yourself by attaching a 'should' to a 'love to'. (I love massages, so I put a back-massager cushion on my writing chair). You should use your cross trainer, but perhaps you prefer reading a book? Get an audiobook and listen to it exclusively while exercising on the machine.

6) Make it a pain to use your unhelpful habit – remove temptation (remove links to FB/Twitter etc. from the work browser or write in desktop word processor without access to the internet; take the batteries out of the remote control; don't carry a credit card if you tend to splurge when stressed/low).

7) Make it super easy to perform your new routine (turn the PC on and find all the supporting materials for work the night before).

8) Ask your friends to help you get started, possibly via Skype support, a buddy for walking or running etc.

9) Reward yourself every time you do what you planned to do e.g. do a happy dance; eat a small piece of dark chocolate (grapes work for me); celebrate with friends, lounge in the hammock in the sunshine.

10) Be kind; forgive yourself for an occasional miss and get back on track the next day or as soon as you think of it! You may have lost one occasion, but you have the rest of your life to think about, so get stuck in and reinforce those useful neural pathways!

Planning, Rituals, and Managing your Time and Energy

If a setback hits you, it is more likely that you will revert to your old habits of thinking and behaviour, and your usual stress and anxiety responses. This is why helpful habits, planning, and happiness-boosting strategies need to go hand-in-hand to make you and your life bulletproof (stress resilient).

Why are planning and pleasure important for befriending stress and reducing anxiety?

Well, you're asking the right question. It is essential for increasing stress resilience via two main benefits:

1) An obvious one, feeling in control and organised, automatically decreases the impact of stress on you;

2) Less obvious is where it lies in your brain – the prefrontal cortex – and how it affects motivation and willpower.

The better your prefrontal cortex works, the easier it is to persevere with helpful habits. Persevering with helpful habits and rituals helps you in a myriad of ways: you achieve your goals, which gives you a mood boost and makes you happier. That reinforces the good habit, making you more likely to repeat the same action next time. However, it also gives you more willpower in other areas of your life, and the more you achieve what you set out to do, the more confident, motivated and less likely to procrastinate you will be.

So basically, we are working on boosting your mood productively to increase motivation and willpower to do what's right. This will help you keep up helpful coping habits and to live the life you want to lead in line with your vision even at the times of challenge. After all, when you are happy and satisfied with your life, it takes a big hit to take you down; but when you're not happy, even minor niggles can feel like insurmountable obstacles.

The prefrontal cortex and pleasure-boosting strategies — taking control

So how do we continue to improve the functioning of the prefrontal cortex to become happier and increase our motivation? Magic! Well, not really! You work on increasing your body's natural ability to produce helpful neurotransmitters such as oxytocin, serotonin, and dopamine:

> • Oxytocin, otherwise known as the 'cuddle hormone', reduces anxiety and encourages your desire to bond with other people and feel empathy towards them;

> • Serotonin helps you to understand what needs to be done because it affects your intuition and perception;

• Dopamine, as mentioned above, is your reward hormone, but it is also related to taking action and control.

Serotonin is an interesting chemical, because it helps to pass signals from one nerve cell to another, so it can really improve the function of your prefrontal cortex, as well as your mood (happiness) and emotion.[47] As a sidenote, it can also disrupt chronic pain signals and how they are sent from one nerve to another. This is why the following strategies are great tools for chronic pain management in addition to being mood boosters. However, the way in which serotonin works isn't entirely understood; even though many antidepressants are believed to work by increasing the amount of serotonin that is present in your blood and brain, or by stopping it from being absorbed and taken apart too quickly. There are natural ways you can help your body towards a mood boost. These can range from taking control, exercising, hugging people, getting a massage,[48] getting more sunlight, recalling happy memories,[49] or through practising gratefulness.

So, let's look at taking control. Any stress and anxiety feels worse when we feel as though we have no control over a situation. However, as you've seen through mindset intervention and taking charge of your habits, you always have a few options. There are small changes that can create a big impact. You can introduce these into

---

[47] NHS Choices (National Health Service, UK). (2016, November 30). Antidepressants. Retrieved January 29, 2017, from http://www.nhs.uk/conditions/Antidepressant-drugs/Pages/Introduction.aspx

[48] Field, T., Hernandez-Reif, M., Diego, M., Schanberg, S., & Kuhn, C. (2005). Cortisol decreases and serotonin and dopamine increase following massage therapy. *The International journal of neuroscience.*, *115*(10), 1397–413. Retrieved from https://www.ncbi.nlm.nih.gov/pubmed/16162447

[49] Korb, A. (2015). Ibid.

your life, boosting your control (or at least the illusion of it, which also works), simultaneously helping you rewire your brain away from unproductive coping habits and towards decisiveness, willpower and a more productive life.

There's no reason to become a control freak to feel that you are in control of your life. You cannot control everything, and it would be a plain waste of energy if you tried. More than 2000 years ago, the Stoics cracked the way to a happier and less anxious life by suggesting that you control (and take action on!) what you can, and ignore or let go of what you can't. The magic trick is in recognising the difference between these two. Focus only on the areas that you can control and trick your brain into feeling in control when it isn't. Remember, we already touched upon disengaging from the unsolvable in the previous chapter.[50]

Taking a look at our brain up close, modern research shows us how different areas in our brain react when we exercise control:

"Making decisions includes creating intentions and setting goals – all three are part of the same neural circuitry and engage the prefrontal cortex in a positive way, reducing worry and anxiety. Making decisions also helps overcome striatum activity, which usually pulls you toward negative impulses and routines. Finally, making decisions changes your perception of the world – finding solutions to your problems and calming the limbic system."[51]

---

[50] Southwick, S. M. & Charney, D. S. (2012). Ibid.

[51] Korb, A. (2015). Ibid.

So, next time you worry or have a problem with something in your life, ask yourself this:

Is this within my control? Can I do something about this?

If the answer is no, then there is no point thinking about all the 'what ifs' and getting into a panic. What you can do, however, is look not at the big picture (panic!) but at the next step; and take the situation step-by-step by only doing what you can at the time. Still panicking? You can give your brain an illusion of control by making any decision you can, because when you make a decision – any decision at all – it engages the prefrontal cortex (your planning centre) and decreases stress and worry. You could even make the decision to worry about it next week, if that is what you preferred to do. That is a decision in itself and it disrupts your brain's habitual worry patterns and gives it an illusion of being in control.

Alternatively, you will need to decide to let go of the problem and focus your attention where you can make a difference. Sometimes, writing things down helps so that you have a reminder – a sort of pointless-to-worry-about list, that you can look at and think, "Yep, it's that and not worth worrying about. Let's move onto something more productive." My mom not willing to give up smoking is one of those things.

If the answer is 'Yes, I can do something about this,' then do something; make a plan, set a goal and execute it; make a change no matter how small it is. By taking control, you will find solutions to your problems, which improve your mood, willpower and positive self-perception and assist with the creation of new, helpful habits. The beauty of decision making and planning is in the rewards you get. If you make a decision, plan a goal and achieve it, you will receive a bigger boost of dopamine than you would if something good simply happened to you by pure luck.[52]

If you struggle with making decisions, give yourself a timeframe in which you must decide and take action. There are often many options and choices we need to make and it can be paralysing to go through them and weighing up the benefits of each of them. After all, you could spend all your life examining the problem (here's me lamenting over the weeds in my garden and the overgrown lawn) and arguing pros and cons of its solution (which lawn mower to get and how to kill the weeds) and doing lots of research instead of living (and end up with a jungle outside my window). So, try to remember that good enough decisions really are good enough. If this is not a life, death or financial ruin kind of situation, give yourself an hour or two to do some research, sum up, discuss with a person close to you and jump in. Your brain will thank you for it!

However, the Stoics also taught that things that happen to us are objective events and it is our perception that makes them either good or bad. In the previous chapter, we learned that we can influence our perception of almost anything in our life and that will affect any decisions we make and actions we take. So instead of buying a lawnmower, I could also choose to see my garden as a wildlife haven and my lawn as a meadow (not a weed-infested jungle).

Rituals, routines, and habit formation

Rituals and routines are fantastic strategies that bring pleasure, peace or comfort, and ensure that tasks get done – every time, on time, properly – and above all, without fuss and uncertainty. When I say rituals, I don't necessarily mean religious ones (e.g. a Catholic person

---

[52] Korb, A. (2015). Ibid. (paraphrased).

making the sign of the cross before praying), although that is where rituals may have originated. Nor do I mean subconscious habits.

To me, rituals are more conscious; unlike habits, they are chosen decisions of how we perform a task, with a focus on the process rather than the outcome. It is our attitude that makes them special, meaningful, fulfilling and engaging.

Routines are similar to rituals, and may also lead to habit formation, but routines have that connotation of mechanical, unvarying behaviour. A routine is a series of events that has an order to it, but the focus is on the outcome rather than the process – the focus is on achieving the task at hand – e.g. my routine for doing the dishes (when I can't use the dishwasher) is:

1) Wash the cleaner things first (glassware);

2) Soak the cutlery in a cup of warm, soapy water;

3) Rinse the crockery roughly;

4) Wash the crockery;

5) Stack the crockery in the draining rack;

6) Rinse the cutlery;

7) Wash the cutlery;

8) Stack the cutlery (sharp points downwards, handles upwards) in the cutlery drainer.

It's unchanging; it's mechanical – it's almost boring, but it ensures things are washed, rinsed and drained properly every time. This is a routine. Other examples of routines are a set of movements in a dance or a set of highly specific functions in a computer program. The emphasis is all about the mechanical performance of a set series of actions; it's not particularly meaningful in and of itself.

Yet, you can transform some routines into enjoyable rituals if you begin to focus on meaning and engagement. It is your attention that makes the difference of whether you get through the dishes mindlessly, without thinking about it. Do you allow your mind to wander or do you choose to pay attention to the moment – to the warmth of the water; the steam rising and swirling in the air; even to the boredom you feel. If your sink has a window above it, you could appreciate the view, the colour of the sky, or the geometry of other buildings in sight. This turns an everyday chore into an enjoyable moment and will make you feel less stressed because you begin to engage with something beyond the mere mechanical nature of the chore.

As Loehr and Schwartz (2004:18) have said: "positive energy rituals – highly specific routines for managing energy – are the key to full engagement and sustained high performance".[53] Creating highly specific routines for different parts of your day is extremely important then. Here's an example of where we established a highly specific ritual in daily life. Lately, we've had a really hard time getting our toddler into bed in the evenings. Dinner was followed by tantrums, many bouts of crying, going to the loo unnecessarily, getting out of bed, calling out to us, etc. Until we have decided not to 'wing' it

---

[53] Schwartz, T., & Loehr, J. E. (2004). *Ibid.*

anymore and we set a predictable, rarely changing, and easy-to-follow ritual that we all enjoy.

Our child's bedtime routine usually consists of:

1) Drink warm cocoa;

2) Fill in reward/star chart with Mummy/Daddy;

3) Brush teeth;

4) Wash face;

5) Go to toilet;

6) Put dirty clothes in laundry basket;

7) Put on pyjamas;

8) Bedtime story;

9) Prayers/reflection on how the day went and what lovely things happened (gratefulness);

10) Hug and kiss, say goodnight.

These ten simple things are done every day, regardless of whether it's the weekend or midweek, or my child is at home or staying at their grandparents' place. This ritual may well (hopefully!) establish habits of good behaviour, health, cleanliness and both spiritual and emotional development. It also establishes the boundary of bedtime, a crucially important concept not just for children, but also for adults. This may take a few weeks or a couple of months to become established (remember those 66 days), but it will become firm over time. If you follow an evening ritual with your child and they go to bed calmly, you can not only enjoy the time with them and create lasting memories, but also instead of fighting them for another half an hour or longer to stay in bed, you can spend half an hour doing something you love or are passionate about. How about reading a favourite book, doing some art or crafts, baking, spending time with your other half, doing a spot of quiet DIY, catching up on the news or skyping your friends?

A bedtime ritual for children is important, as sleep is an essential part of life, but a bedtime routine can apply to adults and is perhaps even more important to reinforce. Sleep helps to heal and restore bodily functions, as well as reinvigorate your mind and process what has happened throughout the day. As adults, it is far too easy, for us to slip into surfing the web, checking social media, watching TV and dealing with a few emails well past 9, 10, or even 11PM. Why is it so important for our kids to be in bed at the right time, but as adults don't practise what we preach? We tell ourselves that we don't need as much sleep. We're adults now; we can just drink coffee (several times daily) to keep ourselves going! But this is, quite simply, dangerous and unhealthy. Although it's very individual, most people need roughly seven or eight hours of quality sleep every night, but what makes us think that we can get away with five or six? It can't go on forever without serious consequences.

Rather than deprive our brains and bodies of necessary recovery time, we need to take a bit of our own medicine and establish good bedtime habits. Create a sleep ritual for yourself[54] that covers all the essentials, just like the child's bedtime routine does. Commit to being in bed at a decent hour, and say no to mobile phones, tablets or other

---

[54] Gascoigne J. (2011, May 8). *Creating a sleep ritual*. Retrieved January 29, 2017, from http://joel.is/creating-a-sleep-ritual/

similar electronics after 9PM. The blue light in the screen will keep your brain active (it blocks the conversion of serotonin into melatonin, an essential hormone that helps you sleep). Even though there are apps out there for filtering out blue light from your devices, if you struggle with getting to sleep, I would advise against using your gadgets, as your brain can still feel activated by the interaction. Instead, try reading a book (it's better to be something unrelated to your work), do some drawing, or build a puzzle in a calmly-lit room.

I have learned to go to sleep by listening to a soothing meditation CD. It took a few months for me to get used to it, going through a body scan and mindful breathing, but now I know that if I put my headphones in and turn the CD on I will be asleep within 5 minutes. Often, I don't even remember more than the first few sentences of the track. It has become a part of my sleep ritual, that I prepare my water bottle, turn my phone to 'no disruptions until the alarm rings', snuggle down and get my mp3 player ready. Knowing that I will be asleep shortly and therefore I'll be able to wake up in the morning without trouble, dissolves my anxieties.

It helps twofold though, to know that being able to wake up when my alarm clock rings, and avoid the continuous 'snooze cycle' gives me extra time the next morning to do what I like to do. To enjoy a nice, hot shower, is essential for dissolving some of my pain and grumpiness, but it also makes me feel clean, fresh and ready for the day. It also gives me extra time to prepare calmly for work and help the rest of the family get ready for their day with me smiling, rather than having a grumpy face.

So you see, having an evening ritual helps us to make space as well as time for activities that are more meaningful, or that simply make us happy. If your ritual is to prepare your work clothes the night before, it only takes you 5 minutes to get dressed in the morning, instead of half an hour. This creates more time for pleasurable things in your life.

Maybe you don't have troublesome toddlers or sleep problems. How about financial pressures? Would you like to be able to cut your food bills in half? You can do this by creating a meal plan for the week (written down so you don't forget) and a correlating shopping list. No more buying stuff you don't know what to do with; no more faffing about and panicking about what's for dinner tonight. If you do create a meal plan and coordinate your shopping, all you need to do when you come home is get your ingredients out, cook, eat and clean up. No need to hunt for recipes only to find out you don't have the right ingredients, and then have to look for another recipe, or dash back out to the shop. You can make this into a ritual by involving your family in meal planning or by taking a quiet moment to do this yourself (with a mug of hot chocolate?).

This can be ritual or routine depending on how much attention you pay to it and how much meaning you find in it. How important or pleasurable it is for you to feed yourself and your family well, save money and have spare time at the end to enjoy.

What do the world's most successful people do?

Don't just take my word for it. Routines and rituals are used by the great and good the world over. They tend to fit into these four themes – meditation, exercise, family, and prayer/gratefulness:

1) Meditation – Both Arianna Huffington and Jack Dorsey (founder of Twitter) get up before 6 AM to meditate. This ritual gives them peace – a great way to start any day;

2) Exercise – Richard Branson and Lord Alan Sugar both exercise first thing in the morning, which puts them in a great mood before cracking on with business;

3) Family Time – Gary Vaynerchuk (the media mogul) hugs his kids for five minutes each morning, and Geoff Bezos (founder of Amazon) avoids morning meetings so he can always have breakfast with his wife;

4) Prayer/Gratefulness – In his autobiography, Benjamin Franklin's morning routine was: 'Rise, wash, and address the Powerful Goodness (God)',[55] and Marky Mark (Mark Wahlberg, the actor, producer, former Calvin Klein model, and businessman) says: "The first thing I do when I start my day is, I get down on my hands and knees and give thanks to God... That 10 minutes helps me in every way throughout the day".[56]

These four activities are powerful rituals that these famous, highly successful people cling to, because they know they are powerful, positive and beneficial to their lives. Maybe we should try to aim for one (or more) of these – whichever has the most meaning to us. which one we value greatly.

Only 24 Hours in the Day? Making Spare Time

Now that we have banished our unhelpful habits and introduced some lovely rituals that have allowed us to free up some space in our

[55] Franklin, B. (1994). *The autobiography of Benjamin Franklin* (3rd ed.). New York: Barnes & Noble Books. Freely available online: https://www.gutenberg.org/files/20203/20203-h/20203-h.htm

[56] Catholic Herald Online. (2017). Mark Wahlberg: "The first thing I do each day is pray" - celebrity news - entertainment - news - Catholic online. Retrieved January 29, 2017, from https://www.catholic.org/news/ae/celebrity/story.php?id=39731

heads, let's get on with making actual time. "But," I hear you say, "I've got no time – no time at all in my day!" Well, it may seem so, but often that's an exaggeration. There is some 'blind time' – time to which we are blind; time we can learn to find and use.

Often, the problem is that we spend time paying attention to things that we think matter (worrying, constantly cleaning, playing video games, watching news, checking our phones again and again). But in the long term, they don't really bring a lot of value to our lives. These activities tend to drain us of mental energy and can sometimes even be quite disempowering. So how do you identify these moments? How do you make space in your day?

Well, start by keeping a diary or a spreadsheet for a few days of how you spend your time. What do you do all day? Where are you likely to claw back a few minutes here and there? Account for every minute in your day – personal hygiene, commuting, putting on make-up, coffee breaks at work, going to the loo ten times because you drank too much coffee at work, TV time, checking your phone or social media (again and again and again), winding down time, mealtimes... Everything counts. I realise that this seems like a lot of work, but it will give you more freedom in the long run.

Often, people find that there are blind spots they haven't considered because they're either too short or they don't occur in their usual environment. That doesn't mean they can't be used in a productive way that brings meaning to life. Are you sitting on the train every day for fifteen minutes playing Clash of Titans? Or checking Facebook? Erm, there is some free time right there. You could even go extreme like Will Smith's character in the movie 'The Pursuit of Happyness' – he tries to avoid hanging around at the water fountain and drinking so that he can have more time to make calls to clients. This meant that he saved time by not nattering to colleagues and didn't waste too much time going to the toilet! I'm not suggesting you dehydrate yourself though; just be mindful and start to notice where you use your time and how productive or useful it is.

Prioritising your time

Maybe your diary is so full that there are no spare minutes anywhere? Try assigning ratings to the activities that you do every day and sort them by meaning, pleasure, and your strengths (1 lowest – 5 highest/best rating):

1) Helping a friend
very meaningful = 5
hard work but pleasurable = 4
my strengths = 5;

2) Working
somewhat meaningful = 3
I earn money = 3
very easy, not using my strengths = 1;

3) Watching TV
not very meaningful = 1
pleasant = 3
didn't require any of my strengths = 1.

Total the points for each activity and rank them from the highest value to the lowest. Prioritise the higher value ones.

The reason why we are rating these in terms of using your strengths is because it is fulfilling and helps grow self-confidence, therefore snowballing into a positive impact over time. Offering your strengths to others has been found to increase happiness and decrease depression.[57]

If rating your current activities didn't get you any closer to spare time, and you're unsure about what really brings meaning to your life, consider what you would really want to do if nobody was judging you. This is a technique offered by Tal Ben-Shahar, lecturer at Harvard University and he suggests: "From now on and for the rest of your life no one will know what you're doing. No one will know about the amazing things that you do for others, no one will know about how rich you are, no one will know about how successful you are, how many people you reach, no one but you alone will know about the things you do. In such a world where a spell of anonymity has been cast on you, what would you do?"[58] This should really help you get to the bottom of who you are, independent from what other people think of you, or who you think you should be.

It is not only important because you need to know what makes you happy and what doesn't, but also because you need to be aware of what you are good at; we all-too-frequently forget to recognise those moments. Understanding what makes you happy will raise your self-confidence and feeling of self-worth and usefulness. It also helps to identify moments of missed opportunities to work on your vision, chances to be happy, and do something for yourself or others.

For some people, mapping things out is not an option, so you may prefer to go with a 'gut feeling' approach. This method is especially

---

[57] Seligman et al. (2005). *Positive psychology progress: Empirical validation of interventions*. American Psychologist. 2005; 60:410–421. [PubMed]

[58] Ben-Shahar, T. (2008). *Happier: Can you learn to be happy?* New York: McGraw-Hill Education - Europe.

relevant to social commitments, invitations to events, and (supposedly) fun activities. It is to go with the 'hell yeah' or 'hell no' theory[59]. If the thought of the commitment doesn't make you go, "Hell yeah, that's amazing and exciting!", then you need to learn to say no, and use the time to do something that *does* make you think, "Hell, yeah!"

This hopefully helps you distinguish between things that do and don't bring value and meaning, those you needn't stress and worry about, and activities and habits that you could replace with something much more YOU! It might take some time to figure out, but it will definitely bring you more satisfaction and happiness and, in turn, the ability to look positively at your life and take control of your situation.

I don't have a single minute to spare!

If you think you *seriously* don't have a single minute spare, the thought of finding time to think about what happened, let alone write it down to find meaning, may not appeal to you. I know how you feel. Sometimes, it can be both mentally and physically challenging to navigate our everyday lives. When did 'normal living' become so stressful? However, the good news is that this busyness isn't always as bad for us as we think. On the contrary, for older people, it seems to be a great predictor for better cognition (learning, reasoning, thinking skills) in later life. A recent study examined 50 – 89-year-olds, and found that: "... greater busyness was associated with better

[59] Sivers, D. (2009, August 26). No "yes." either "HELL YEAH!" or "no." | Derek Sivers. Retrieved January 29, 2017, from https://sivers.org/hellyeah

processing speed, working memory, episodic memory, reasoning, and crystallised knowledge".[60]

Another recent study, showed that if we choose to help others when we feel pressured for time, we start to feel less pressured. We have the total opposite outcome! "Participants who gave time felt as though they had more time".[61] So how about a little challenge? Help others when you feel overwhelmed. If you can't possibly stop doing everything and still feel very busy, try to go with the flow. If nothing else, all this research has shown us is that **it is *how* we face the challenges that matters, not *how many* of these challenges there are.** So we should be proud of what we achieve, but work towards appropriate rest breaks in which we can recharge our mental and physical energy.

I never have any plans for my day

Are you on the opposite side of the spectrum, thinking, "I've got no plans again today, I will be bored, and lonely, and will probably just veg in front of the telly all day,"? Then learn to say, "Why not?!" to new experiences, even if you don't particularly feel excited about them at the time. Have you been invited to a New Year's party by an acquaintance? Or is there an ice skating rink in your town? Have you seen a poster for a quiz night at the local social club? Have no other plans? Why not? It might just turn out to be more fun than you

---

[60] Festini, S. B., McDonough, I. M., & Park, D. C. (2016). The busier the better: Greater busyness is associated with better Cognition., *8*,. Retrieved from https://www.ncbi.nlm.nih.gov/pmc/articles/PMC4870334/

[61] Mogilner, C., Chance, Z., & Norton, M. (2012). Giving time gives you time. *Psychological science.*, *23*(10), 1233–8. Retrieved from https://www.ncbi.nlm.nih.gov/pubmed/22972905

expect: meeting new people, learning new things and growing as a person.

Prioritising your time is extremely important, but prioritising your energy may be even more critical. In the examples earlier, about the rituals of famous people, there were four themes – meditation, exercise, family, and prayer. These four areas gave strength to each of the people mentioned – mental, physical, emotional, and spiritual strength. They are the four areas highlighted by Schwartz and Loehr[62] in which you can – and should, mobilise your energy resources. Interestingly, their research originally began with tennis players, then broadened to include other sportspeople, and finally opened up to anyone. As I mentioned way back in the beginning, tennis players such as Serena Williams not only seek out stress (applying a growth mindset towards it), but they also make use of mini-breaks for energy recovery. To perform to a high standard, it is necessary for each of us to engage each of the four areas – mental, physical, emotional, and spiritual – and not only exercise, but recover in each of them. These four sources of energy are said to be the fundamental building blocks of your daily rhythms for activity and rest. Pay attention to each, and they will pay you back in dividends for life.

Now that we have started to organise our time and energy, and have gotten our brains working to our advantage, let's focus on the things that really matter. Let's focus on what makes us happy, which in turn will increase motivation; focus on those that incite passion, which in turn improves life satisfaction!

Because all of this brings out the most resilient you.

---

[62] Schwartz, T., & Loehr, J. E. (2004). Ibid.

Summary of Chapter 3:

• Free up mental space by creating helpful coping habits, routines and rituals.

• In challenging situations, acknowledge your coping habits. If not helpful, replace them.

• Make a start with a keystone habit that will snowball the positive effects on your life.

• Repeat and reward the new habit. Your dopamine hits will be quicker and motivation higher.

• Become resilient through taking control, planning and increasing motivation.

• Meaningful rituals lead to success.

• Prioritising helps you get busy with what really matters!

Chapter 4. Focus, Happiness and Relationships: Bringing out the Resilient You

<u>Keywords</u>
Being sociable
Engaging oxytocin
Boosting happiness and motivation
Hormones (serotonin, dopamine, endorphins)
Mindfulness
(Re)discovering your passions
Maintaining change and challenge

So far, we have learned about:

- what stress is, and what it isn't;

- your mindset and why it's so important;

- how to realise your values; and

- taking control by implementing structure, rituals and meaningful practices in your life.

Hopefully, I have already managed to change your mind about stress, helped you discover that stress and anxious feelings are not always your enemy, and that you can make stress work for you. You can use it to fuel your performance with energy for positive impact, as well as help you lead a happier, more meaningful, and healthier life.

You've learned about starting to take control of your life and introducing more helpful habits and rituals in order to make mental space and free up time, so that we can recharge as well as give time for pleasure and meaning. With the help of our daily habits, rituals and routines, we have established a good foundation – a strong framework on which we can build, and within which we can develop as a person and progress to bringing out our most resilient selves.

We have already touched upon focus in the previous chapter when we talked about the difference between a routine (performing tasks without paying attention, focussing on the outcome) and ritual (mindful practice, focussing on the process). We now look at focus as paying attention to ourselves, to our surroundings, and to our relationships. In this chapter, we will also see how attention and relationships disarm the effects of stress on our bodies and carry us through the most difficult situations. We will cover:

- Relationships – How social life affects stress; how relationships and helping others/volunteering ultimately help us too, by disarming the damaging effects of stress;

- Attention through mindfulness – what it is, and how it can help us;

- Practical resilience-building strategies and focussing on our experience:

- Compassion – not just for others, but also towards ourselves;

- Happiness – how to observe our own moments of happiness;

- Living through your passions;

- Being grateful;

- Paying attention to positives and what matters most;

- Growing and challenging yourself – motivate yourself like an athlete.

Relationships

One of the biggest predictors of how well we handle stress in our lives is the quality of our support network. We have already touched upon various stress responses, but the one most closely affecting our relationships is the one described as a 'tend and befriend' response. "The 'tend and befriend' theory builds on the observation that human beings affiliate in response to stress. Under conditions of threat, they tend to offspring to ensure their survival and affiliate with others for joint protection and comfort".[63]

So 'tending' means caring for children, family, friends, partners or even organisations (charities, churches, communities, clubs). Befriending encompasses building social ties, such as listening to people in need, being there for others, and supporting them through difficult times. We have already mentioned in previous chapters that the neurotransmitter/hormone oxytocin is thought to be the mechanism underlying this response, which can affect our brains as well as our bodies.[64]

---

[63] Taylor, S. E. in Kruglanski, A. W., Higgins, T. E., & Paul A. M. van Lange (Eds.). (2011). *Handbook of theories of social psychology*. London, United Kingdom: SAGE Publications. Available online: https://taylorlab.psych.ucla.edu/wp-content/uploads/sites/5/2014/11/2011_Tend-and-Befriend-Theory.pdf

[64] Taylor, S. E., Klein, L. C., Lewis, B. P., Gruenewald, T. L., Gurung, R. A. R., & Updegraff, J. A. (2000). Biobehavioral responses to stress in females: Tend-and-

McGonigal[65] describes how it helps us act with compassion in times of stress to help others, even if there may be a danger to ourselves, and how this makes us braver. It makes us seek social support and inclusion, thereby avoiding isolation. Although the 'tend and befriend' response is more prevalent in women than in men[66] and it can be more woman-to-woman oriented (Taylor et al. 2000, ibid), in both sexes, it downregulates the effects of stress on the brain[67] as well as on the cardiovascular system.[68] It helps to open our arteries and veins, and prevent or reverse the negative effects of stress on our health (McGonigal, 2015, ibid.).

We can choose and practise tending and befriending, even if it isn't entirely natural for us to do so, whether we are male or female. Irrespective of whether our usual response is fight, flight, freeze or isolate, we can remember to make a conscious effort to reach out to our friends, families, co-workers or support groups. You can create an action plan for stressful situations. Write down 3 things you know that will help you deal with it and as soon as you realise you are feeling

---

befriend, not fight-or-flight. Psychological Review, 107(3), 411–429. doi:10.1037//0033-295x.107.3.411

[65] McGonigal, K. (2015). The upside of stress: Why stress is good for you (and how to get good at it). London, United Kingdom: Vermilion.

[66] Tamres, L. K., Janicki, D., & Helgeson, V. S. (2002). Sex differences in coping behavior: A Meta-Analytic review and an examination of relative coping. Personality and Social Psychology Review, 6(1), 2–30. doi:10.1207/s15327957pspr0601_1

[67] Inagaki, T. K., Bryne Haltom, K. E., Suzuki, S., Jevtic, I., Hornstein, E., Bower, J. E., & Eisenberger, N. I. (2016). The Neurobiology of giving versus receiving support. Psychosomatic Medicine, 78(4), 443–453. doi:10.1097/psy.0000000000000302

[68] Schreier, H. M. C., Schonert-Reichl, K. A., & Chen, E. (2013, April 1). Effect of volunteering on risk factors for cardiovascular disease in Adolescents A Randomized controlled trial. Retrieved January 29, 2017, from JAMA Pediatrics, http://jamanetwork.com/journals/jamapediatrics/fullarticle/1655500

under pressure, use your plan. Mine are: socialise; exercise; and pamper (very similar to when I have a painful flare-up, actually). In a way, when not under stress, we can all turn this around and "**bank social support**" in order to boost our emotional resilience and social safety net for the future.

You can do this by helping others and investing yourself in enhancing and building your social network. You can volunteer, join interest groups, or simply arrange to regularly meet and chat with your friends and family. This not only makes you feel better because you release more oxytocin, but it also challenges you, gets you out there, builds your confidence, and helps build a safety net for the future. The focus here is on being genuinely interested in, and offering support to, others for as long as you can. After all, Dale Carnegie said:

> **"You can make more friends in two months by becoming interested in other people than you can in two years by trying to get other people interested in you."[69]**

By being there for others, you will also reap rewards such as better health and living a longer and happier life. Susan Pinker says in The Village Effect: "if you're surrounded by a tightly connected circle of friends who regularly gather to eat and share gossip, you'll not only have fun but you're also likely to live an average of fifteen years longer than a loner."[70]

It isn't only longevity that is affected by prosocial behaviour (helping others and supporting them in times of need). It also decreases some inflammation markers and lowers cholesterol (Schreier et al. 2013,

[69] Carnegie, D. (1937). *How to win friends and influence people*. New York: New York, Simon and Schuster [c1964].

[70] Pinker, S. (2014). *The village effect: How face-to-face contact can make us healthier, happier, and smarter*. United States: Tantor Media.

ibid.). But let's be honest, time is an issue and we do spend an awful lot of it online. Unless you use this time to arrange face-to-face meetings, it only leads to more isolation and less time with family and friends.[71] Although it sometimes feels like it is becoming more difficult to have close relationships in our present time, you can still build and cherish strong bonds through your friends, family, community, support groups, co-workers, and other like-minded people. No matter how stressed, unwell, or exhausted you feel, there is always something you can give – be it your time, a listening ear, your expertise, a hug, or simply your presence. Arnstein and colleagues (2002) have shown that even people who are personally suffering from chronic pain can offer effective peer support and benefits to others – improvements in pain, disability and depression, "outweighed any frustrations experienced by volunteers".[72]

You might be thinking, "Seriously, sometimes I feel like I don't even have time to tie my shoelaces, let alone help others!" Well, when we think we are stressed and pushed for time, we can become selfish, defensive, and feel like we simply do not have enough hours in the day to get all our stuff done. This is actually a fight-or-flight response. But it turns out that this does not have to be the case. In the previous chapter, we mentioned a study (Mogilner et al., 2012, ibid.) that demonstrated that if we choose to help others when we feel pressured for time, we have the opposite outcome. We feel better, more relaxed, and as if we have *more* time! We use the 'tend and

---

[71] Kraut, R., Patterson, M., Lundmark, V., Kiesler, S., Mukopadhyay, T., & Scherlis, W. (1998). Internet paradox. A social technology that reduces social involvement and psychological well-being? *The American psychologist.*, *53*(9), 1017–31. Retrieved from https://www.ncbi.nlm.nih.gov/pubmed/9841579

[72] Arnstein, P., Vidal, M., Wells-Federman, C., Morgan, B., & Caudill, M. (2002). From chronic pain patient to peer: Benefits and risks of volunteering. *Pain Management Nursing*, *3*(3), 94–103. doi:10.1053/jpmn.2002.126069

befriend' response to feel better. We feel more competent to handle what is on our plate than we did before we helped others. Remember the keystone habits? They change how you see yourself and their effect snowballs over time. Well, being generous with your time (amongst other things) helps release oxytocin, which makes you feel good *and* connected. Not only does it increase your feelings of self-worth and self-confidence, but it also helps you become more emotionally resilient for the future. "A long line of empirical research, including one study of over 2,000 people, has shown that acts of altruism—giving to friends and strangers alike—decrease stress and strongly contribute to enhanced mental health."[73] Wow, being more sociable is awesome! So how do we become more socially connected?

You have already made space in your head through introducing helpful habits and rituals. You have also created more space in your life by prioritising, and deciding on, what constitutes the most meaningful and valuable use of your time. Now, try following your interests into new social environments. Are you into knitting, football, or fermenting your own beer? Whatever you're interested in, there will either be a group in your city, or at least an online forum devoted to it. From there, you can start meeting like-minded people or discussing your favourite topics with them online. One thing I often struggled with as a parent of young children was getting to interest groups. I legitimately didn't have the energy to go out in the evening, especially after a full day of caring for my children. However, there was no shortage of babies' and children's activity groups going on in my local area at various times of day. So, I went to those. I went to a

---

[73] Achor, S. (2010). *The happiness advantage: The seven principles of positive psychology that fuel success and performance at work*. New York: Crown Publishing Group.

group almost every day from when my first child was about 3-4 months old. To be totally honest with you, at first, I *really* hated it; I genuinely loathed the idea of going. I mean, I didn't know anyone – *anyone*! And everyone else was weird (obviously because I am the only *normal* person on the planet); but I just kept going. I started to recognise the odd person and realise that they lived on the next street, or that we were in antenatal class together, but we hadn't spoken to each other because I was way too shy and embarrassed. I even used to schedule events back-to-back so that I couldn't stay and talk to anyone after any meeting – that's how shy I was.

The relative safety of these groups, in which most people are going through similar issues, allowed me to develop my self-confidence. After a while, things changed. I had somehow managed to form a new habit, after repeated practice of this new going-to-groups behaviour. It's a keystone habit that allowed me to make the most of all kinds of encounters. I learned to talk to anyone I met at the playground or even those I bumped into on the street (no, I'm not kidding, I actually ended up making friends with a lady who was blocking my path as she moved into her new house). I now have a large network of people who are in the same position as me, or who are rather different to me but they're very interesting, lovely people; and they live nearby. Their children play with mine and go to each other's birthday parties. I am privileged to count some of these people as close friends (including the path-blocker!) and they are truly a great blessing in my life, something for which I am *very* grateful.

It truly was *not* easy to make friends with all these new people at first, but it got easier over time after the repeated practice helped me to form that useful habit. I also recognised that we had some similarities, shared interests, shared experiences, or even all of the above. I am definitely a happier person because of this, so I am confident that you will have the same outcome if you stick with a positive, new, social habit. The beginnings might be a little tricky, but remember – it's a challenge and it will make your life more awesome if you stay with it!

Choosing something that's close to your heart and circumstances is fantastic and easy to keep doing; but what is the thing that brings the most reward – the most satisfaction in life? Studies[74] have shown that our sense of **well-being and contentedness goes up if we aim for goals that are greater than our own personal desires.** As a bonus, the likelihood of becoming depressed goes down. So, tap into your inner happiness and stress resilience by volunteering. If you have identified a bit of spare time every so often, you can be generous with your time and attention by volunteering at events, or for organisations in which you are interested. Again, this works in the same way as making friends from interest groups, but you will also get that **warm and fuzzy feeling through the release of oxytocin,** because you're volunteering for something bigger than yourself. You are helping others as well as being part of a tribe (interest group). 'Greater than self' goals and acts of participation are extremely beneficial to you, in addition to the people you're helping. As mentioned previously, research shows benefits above and beyond mental health, which include: increased longevity, a decreased likelihood of stress-related death, lower blood pressure, a decrease in feelings of depression and loneliness, and relief from chronic pain (this has been mentioned in several studies, including Schreier et al., 2013, ibid. and Arnstein et al., 2002, ibid.) "Helping others predicted reduced mortality

---

[74] Crocker, J., Olivier, M.-A., & Nuer, N. (2009). Self-image goals and compassionate goals: Costs and benefits. , *8*(2-3), . Retrieved from http://www.ncbi.nlm.nih.gov/pmc/articles/PMC3017354/

specifically by buffering the association between stress and mortality."[75]

Finding the above pieces of research helped me put into words how I felt when I became involved in a support group for people with chronic invisible illnesses. I knew I was feeling better and less lonely, but I also realised that I suddenly had more purpose in my life. I was not focussing solely on my (and my family's) immediate needs or my anxieties about the future. I was also helping others progress with their lives, listening to their issues, and lending a hand where I could. My pain didn't go away, but my view of it has changed. From the pain being under the microscope and always in the forefront of my mind, bugging me, it has since become my helper, because it helped me relate to others. Therefore, the unpleasant experience of chronic pain and stress became a source of togetherness with other members of the support group. Consequently, my social support network grew and now whenever any one of us is going through a tough time, there's always another member there who understands and can help.

I would like to give you one more reason not to avoid stress altogether. Not just because it can give you energy, motivate you, and make you see what's important – but also because it makes your life fuller. If you avoid stress altogether, your life becomes diminished, because you are narrowing down your experiences. Remember the example from above, where I hated going to baby groups? My life was made smaller by my fears and resulting stress about meeting other parents. After I started going to the groups, I gradually made friends

[75] Poulin, M. J., Brown, S. L., Dillard, A. J., & Smith, D. M. (n.d.). Giving to others and the association between stress and mortality. , 103(9), . Retrieved from https://www.ncbi.nlm.nih.gov/pmc/articles/PMC3780662/

and my life is better because of it. I have more help and support if, and when, I need it, and my kids have a variety of friends that are different to their schoolmates. Accepting, and even embracing your situation, could be the key to leading a more abundant life. The importance lies in how you approach your source of stress – and there is one powerful technique that I'd like to talk about that could really help you in a variety of high-pressure situations.

Attention through Mindfulness

Trying to get away from stress and anxiety creates a form of resistance (and for many people, physical and emotional pain) which is natural to us. However, a better approach is to draw closer to the stress we are experiencing, by paying close attention to it and examining it gently and consciously. We may then realise that the impact of the situation changes in front of our eyes – after all, primary suffering (pain or stress) is part of life, but secondary suffering (i.e. how you react to it) is largely our own doing.[76] Penman et al. speak of an injured child and how you would embrace them even if you can't change their suffering. If you can't change the stress and anxiety you feel, although counterintuitive, mindfulness teaches you to become closer to this experience. It also shows you how to be compassionate to yourself and others, and to accept that these feelings exist and they come in and out of existence as you breathe in and out.

You wouldn't want to abandon a hurting child, just as you cannot abandon your hurting body or mind – regardless of whether you feel pain, stress, or anxiety. Instead, uou stay, comfort your body and

---

[76] Penman, D., Burch, V., & IVONNE, P. (2013). *Mindfulness for Health: A practical guide to relieving pain, reducing stress and restoring wellbeing.* London: Little, Brown Book Group.

mind, and know that as life changes, you want to pay attention to every moment. You wouldn't want to forget the first time your child fell off a bike because they hurt themselves; you would want to be there for them and remember the moment for what it was – a once-in-a-lifetime experience. So be there for yourself; be kind and non-judgmental. It is an experience – and one that will pass, at that. Many times, by practising, you will find that the impact of your experiences is likely to change for the better if you find yourself able to approach them with kindness and compassion.

Talking about mindfulness is not just a current fad. It's a practice which is thousands of years old. Although most people recognise it as a Buddhist tradition, it spans many cultures in slightly varying forms. It is a meditative practice, a way of paying attention to your thought life; and it can be used in various religious or cultural traditions without conflicting or undermining one's personal beliefs. Mindfulness is very simple to get started with from the comfort of your own home. But first, I'll just give you a quick overview.

Mindfulness is not some wishy-washy, new-age, or Far East practice; rather, it is essentially about being very conscious and aware in the moment. The more focussed you are on the moment, situation, or experience, the more you will notice about yourself. You become more aware of your own feelings – both physical and emotional, as well as your thoughts and any other sensations you may notice in your body, without judging them. You don't beat yourself up about things. Therefore, we might summarise mindfulness as being very aware and focussed on what is happening in and around you, without developing a narrative explanation for it. This practice allows you to experience positive, as well as negative, effects in a more level-headed way; where you slow down a bit, enabling you to choose to react to negative stimuli or choose to let go.

"To let go means to give up coercing, resisting, or struggling, in exchange for something more powerful and wholesome which comes out of allowing things to be as they are without getting caught up in your attraction to or rejection of them..."
(Jon Kabat-Zinn)[77]

Mindfulness is helpful because it allows us more freedom to feel and see what is there right in front of us – without resistance, tension, or avoidance; without getting tangled in our likes and dislikes; without letting our brain run away with our thoughts. It teaches us to acknowledge what's going on, and then let go of it without falling into anger or frustration. Mindfulness therefore releases the mental tension that can arise from our undisciplined brain thinking about the negatives in our lives, or inventing unhelpful, disempowering narratives about our situation. It can consequently help us become more mentally disciplined and achieve greater concentration. It is particularly helpful when we have habits of avoidance, because it teaches us to focus on something and just experience it, rather than run away from it. Thus, mindfulness is often used as a therapeutic technique, as it can help to address ongoing habits, phobias, and difficult or painful situations (MBSR – mindfulness-based stress reduction).

Mindfulness is also especially helpful if you are struggling with relationships, or have some social angst. Rather than believing everything the left side of your brain interprets about a situation, mindfulness helps you pay more attention to the inputs coming towards the right side of your brain. For example, imagine that you're

---

[77] Kabat-Zinn, J. (2004). *Wherever you go, there you are: Mindfulness meditation for everyday life*. London: Piatkus Books.

having lunch with your friends, who are not looking happy. Some people would then start listening to their left brain, which might say: 'It's because that risotto you made is gross; you're a terrible cook, and you should never have attempted to make risotto." However, if you focus on the messages being transmitted from your right brain, it might go something like this: "Your friends look unhappy; you feel cold; you're eating risotto; this wine tastes good; this wine is a pleasant, chilled temperature." Because you're focussing on these facts, rather than narratives[78] invented by your left brain to link your feelings, external stimuli, and actions together, you will be able to notice that it's cold and that the chilled wine is making you feel colder. Then, you'd realise that you didn't switch the heating on; you might then realise that this could be the reason why your friends look a bit unhappy. It isn't because you're a terrible host and can't cook risotto! It's because you have nice, polite friends who didn't want to trouble you to fire up the heating. Heating is expensive, and you have already gone to the trouble of preparing them a delicious risotto. You even bought a nice wine and chilled it to the perfect temperature!

See, mindfulness is *very* cool. Speaking of risotto, you can also use mindfulness for dieting or trying to cultivate better eating habits. Again, it's about not listening as much to the left side of your brain, but concentrating on the facts and physical sensations, and being curious about all the raw data flowing to your right brain. Here's an example – when you sit down to eat, close your eyes. Focus on the

---

[78] I spoke of this narrative-forming habit back in chapter 1, when I discussed explanatory style. Some of us tend to lean towards a negative way of thinking, which means that our self-created narratives lean towards negative explanations of the facts. Mindfulness helps to reduce or eliminate the negative, let's say, judgemental narratives we sometimes tell ourselves.

fact that you are about to eat. Breathe in and notice the different aromas – spicy, earthy, deep tomato smell, mmm. Sense the warmth of the food rising towards your face. Think about what you are about to be eating, and why. Think about the ingredients, and how they got to you. Slowly open your eyes, and look at your food. Notice how your eyes react to the food, pay attention to how you feel right now – excited, happy, relieved, grateful – whatever you feel. Acknowledge the feeling, but don't dwell on it; just accept it and then move on. Slowly eat the first bite and then savour the moment – every movement around your mouth, how the food feels, how it tastes, whether it has any aftertaste or residual mouthfeel. This process sounds long-winded, but it needn't last ages. Remember, your brain works at ludicrous speed; it's the fastest computer on the planet! A few moments of reflection on the diverse aspects of our food can help us eat with more thought; thus, we find ourselves eating less when we may previously tended to overindulge, and we are more likely to eat healthier if we have previously lacked in that area.

Food is just an easy, everyday example, but one of the main areas with which mindfulness can help is with beating stress. Since we know that stress is not our enemy, running away from it is not necessary. Earlier, I discussed embracing those things that cause our stress, and realising that we get only worked up about something because we care about it. These realisations are a great foundation towards applying mindfulness to the relief of stress and anxiety – if we focus on something in order to accept and embrace it, we will gain a deeper understanding – not only of ourselves, but also of the situation at hand that is generating our stress.

Let's use another example, this time from the workplace – you're at your desk and your boss is approaching. You become a little nervous and realise you haven't finished the monthly figures yet. Your boss gets closer and closer and you become more and more anxious that she's going to talk about those figures you haven't done... You start to think, "It's probably because I'm going to get fired. I'm a terrible employee anyway; why did they even hire me?" STOP! Just wait. Just breathe. Silently name what you're feeling (remember the emotion labelling exercise?) – a little anxiety. Notice how the hairs on the back of your neck are standing up, and how you are breathing? Most likely your breathing is a little quicker than usual. Notice the pen in your hand – you're tapping the end of it rather quickly. These simple tactics slow the moment down and help you to re-focus on the present, rather than pre-living a future that may not happen anyway.

Again, we are using the right brain instead of automatically accepting the left's narrative interpretation of what's happening. It's a bit like being there for yourself in a moment of worry – instead of someone tapping on your shoulder telling you it's going to be alright, you slow your own moment down so you notice what you're doing and how you are reacting. Then you can calm yourself, prepare, or smile in advance.

"You can't stop the waves, but you can learn to surf"
(Jon Kabat-Zinn)[79]

Mindfulness can be applied to a myriad of situations that bring about stress or anxiety, but it's important to remember that it's neither a cure-all, nor a fad – and using it won't bring about world peace. Some call it a way of life and some use it occasionally, as the need arises. Whichever way you choose, be aware that to reap the most

---

[79] Kabat-Zinn, J., A quote by Jon Kabat-Zinn. Retrieved January 31, 2017, from http://www.goodreads.com/quotes/331826-you-can-t-stop-the-waves-but-you-can-learn-to

benefits, you will need to practise your new technique of mindfulness conscientiously and regularly.

If sitting still and watching the world go by doesn't appeal to you, you can try active mindfulness through this challenge:

A month in pictures:

> • Take a photograph every day of anything you find interesting or beautiful;

> • If you do it outdoors, you can combine activity, exercise and exploration;

If you take pictures indoors, explore form, colours, texture, and what is or isn't shown. Taking pictures daily makes you pay more attention to the moment and to your surroundings, as well as to the beauty and strangeness of the world.[80]

Compassion

World peace might be a stretch, but a way to achieve peace of mind might be closer than you think. You can use techniques like mindfulness to achieve practical things through which you can improve your life, such as the healthy eating example mentioned above. It is a fantastic and useful tool. It can help with how we treat ourselves in very stressful moments, but also in everyday life and in getting through those daily struggles we sometimes face. We do beat ourselves up about things sometimes, don't we?! *Yet there is no need to be so hard on yourself.* Mindfulness can help us cultivate compassion towards ourselves (and others), if we're not already that

---

[80] For further information on mindfulness, look into the work of Jon Kabat-Zinn, quoted above, founder of the Mindfulness-Based Stress Reduction Clinic at the University of Massachusetts Medical School: http://www.umassmed.edu/cfm/

way inclined. We are all human and live side-by-side with over 7 billion people on this planet. Some are like us; some are very different – but we don't need to compare ourselves. We need to recognise that everyone is on their *own journey* in life; a journey of discovery about who they are, what they're capable of, and how much of a precious and amazing gift life really is. Some people don't even realise that they're on that journey yet!

Once we recognise for ourselves that there is a whole world of opportunity out there, irrespective of our background, we can start living and giving in a compassionate and abundant way. It helps us feel more fulfilled, and helps others to achieve this feeling too. But it needs to start with ourselves first. We are truly unique, beautiful creations and we should value this life we have.

As human beings, we are capable of overcoming so much, and we should tell ourselves that every day! Just like we discussed in the last chapter, we should incorporate this positivity as part of our daily rituals. A little bit of mindfulness, carefully applied, can help us ease up and judge ourselves less. We can, instead, be gently curious about what is going on in and around us, and in and around the lives of others.

By removing the often damaging and incorrect narratives formulated by our left brain, we can go easy on ourselves, and then understand that other people go through trials and tribulations just like we do. We are more like others than we realise; but we often have the tendency to think that everyone else has a better life, or they have it easy because they're richer, better-looking, or more educated than we perceive ourselves to be.

> **"If one only wished to be happy, this could be easily accomplished; but we wish to be happier than other**

people, and this is always difficult, for we believe
others to be happier than they are".
(Charles de Montesquieu)[81]

This comparison narrative isolates us. Yet, we are not alone, because everyone's brain does this! Therefore, thinking in a focussed way, as mindfulness teaches us to do, makes it easier to have compassion for others as well. Compassion makes it easier for us to get closer to people who are dealing with painful or sad situations. This is the root of relationships and helping others – you are narrowing the gap of isolation between yourself and the other person, which is a beautiful, even necessary practice that we could all do a lot more. Essentially, through being mindful towards others' situations, we become more compassionate, and we can help to lessen the power of isolating narratives of another person and not just ourselves, helping them as well as ourselves in the process.

Compassion for others is wonderful, and helping to understand them is all great. It helps us build effective social support networks, but what about our own personal happiness in life? Aside from the benefits of compassion, using mindfulness can also help us observe our own moments of happiness and monitor their frequency. Because all too often, we barely notice them. We glance over them and run after the next thing that might make us happy, so we don't notice how often we even are happy.

Happy moments don't last forever. We have our ups and downs, but we can make the ups last longer, and make them more frequent. We

---

[81] Edwards, T. (1908). *A dictionary of thoughts: Being a Cyclopedia of Laconic quotations from the best authors of the world, Both ancient and modern.* Retrieved from https://books.google.co.uk/books?id=zlMxAAAAIAAJ&redir_esc=y

do this by simply taking the time to observe these moments of happiness with full attention. Notice what we feel during those times. Labelling your emotions and physical feelings may help clarify the moment. Were we happiest when having a very participatory experience? Or watching something from a distance? Was our happy time full of adrenaline when racing downhill on a mountain bike? Or did we well up with emotion when receiving a picture our little child gave us? Did we feel a quiet, peaceful calm and contentedness when watching our kids play together across the room?

If we learn to focus on what is unfolding in us, physically and emotionally, in different types of situations, we'll easily discover what makes us happy. From there, it's an easy step to make those situations more frequent and longer. For example, I recently started having lunch with a friend once a week. Whilst she was talking to me about some childhood memories, I applied mindfulness techniques to the situation, and realised that I was very happy. I was letting my soup go cold, but I was enjoying the moment so much that the cold soup didn't matter. I enjoyed seeing her have the freedom to talk about her past and I could tell she was enjoying reminiscing about specific memories, too. It made me realise that spending intimate quality time with a close friend was a deep source of happiness to me, something I hadn't previously understood about myself. I always enjoyed group gatherings of friends and work colleagues; but now that I know something more about myself, I can plan more one-to-one times with a friend, thereby increasing my happiness, as well as developing that particular friendship in its own right.

Mindfulness is also very good at helping us understand what makes us unhappy. One of the things I noticed in my own life was how sad, angry, depressed, frustrated, and annoyed I became whilst watching the news. I observed that whenever I focussed my attention on it, I felt worse 99% of the time. I only felt better when I watched the sports headlines, because I enjoy watching and playing sports. So, I decided to stop watching the main news. All that negativity going into my eyes and brain was making me unhappy. Instead, I made a conscious decision to watch a football match instead.

Happiness

Happiness: living for your passions and challenging yourself to grow

As you can see, happiness is not the elusive final reward for all that you have accomplished. I didn't plan that cold soup moment with my friend; I just discovered the happiness that was there all along. You don't need to wait for your goals to be accomplished so you can be happy. You are able to see that happiness is always with you, around you, and sometimes right in front of your nose – and you have the power to make it flourish. **Happiness is the *prerequisite* for your success and life satisfaction, rather than the *outcome* of these.**

Humans tend to think that whatever is behind the next corner will make them happier: the next job; the next pair of shoes; the new house; not having to work (or returning to work); having more money; having less money; having more time; having fewer worries etc. But already in the 70s, research[82] showed that we adapt to all situations. Whether these have a positive or negative impact, our level of happiness increases only temporarily until we become used to the new situation, when our mood returns to its usual level (called

---

[82] Brickman, P., Coates, D., & Janoff-Bulman, R. (1978). Lottery winners and accident victims: Is
happiness relative? Journal of Personality and Social Psychology, 36, 917-927

a happiness set point).[83] This is called a hedonic (happiness) adaptation or sometimes a happiness treadmill. This mechanism is very useful when dealing with negative events on your life, such as when dealing with the adverse effects of medical issues. However, the happiness treadmill appears to be an impediment, rather than a help to our pursuit of happiness.

It is not our pursuit of things and 'better situations' that makes us happier though. We can genuinely choose to be happy now, regardless of our possessions or circumstances in life, and we can be content throughout any situation in which we find ourselves. There are studies that have proven that your happiness now is extremely significant in influencing your future success.

> "If we can get somebody to raise their levels of optimism or deepen their social connection or raise happiness, [it] turns out every single business and educational outcome we know how to test for improves dramatically. You can increase your success rates for the rest of your life and your happiness levels will flatline, but if you raise your level of happiness and deepen optimism it turns out every single one of your success rates rises dramatically compared to what it would have been at negative, neutral, or stressed."[84]

---

83 Lykken, D., & Tellegen, A. (1996). HAPPINESS IS A STOCHASTIC PHENOMENON. Psychological Science, 7(3), 186–189. doi:10.1111/j.1467-9280.1996.tb00355.x

84 Oregon State University. (2016, May 4). New Harvard research reveals a fun way to be more successful. Retrieved January 30, 2017, from http://sli.oregonstate.edu/feature-story/new-harvard-research-reveals-fun-way-be-more-successful

Lyubomirsky et al. (2005)[85] have proposed that the wellbeing and happiness of individuals were affected by three major factors: genetic predisposition (a happiness set point – approx. 50%); life circumstances (marital status, income, religion – approx. 10%); and most importantly, cognitive, behavioral, and goal-based activities. These can account for up to 40% of wellbeing and happiness. However, there is a new school of thought that believes that it is possible to override your genes by changing your mindset and habits, and increasing positivity in your daily life.

> "Most people accept that they're just born some way and that's how they're going to be the rest of their life, and whatever they were last year is what they're going to be this year. I think positive psychology shows us that that doesn't actually have to be the case."[86]

So, remember your growth mindset! People can change and so can you!

I discussed in the second chapter how your positive outlook, as well as finding meaning, is very important for leading a healthy life with the help of – and sometimes in spite of – stress and anxiety. Feeling happier helps with this through increasing your emotional resilience. There are many strategies that can help you along the way:

- Living through your passions;

---

[85] Lyubomirsky, S., Sheldon, K. M., & Schkade, D. (2005). Pursuing happiness: The architecture of sustainable change. *Review of General Psychology, 9*(2), 111–131. doi:10.1037/1089-2680.9.2.111

[86] Achor, S. (2010) Ibid.

- Being grateful;

- Paying attention to positives and what matters most;

- Growing and challenging yourself.

So, if you need a little bit more happiness, here is how to get it:

Passions/meaning – life satisfaction

Live through your passions and purpose to gain a lifelong, lasting satisfaction.

When we do what we are passionate about, it increases meaning in our lives. It makes us more courageous when dealing with setbacks and ultimately brings satisfaction. "That's all well and good," you say, "but I've been so stressed for ages, I don't even know what my passions are!" That's fine. There are several ways to locate your passions, and these are dependent on the way you function as a person. If you know yourself well and are quite an imaginative person, picture your future self leading an ideal life. What would this life be like? Would it be very similar to your current life, but with tiny adjustments such as shorter work hours or a different work task? Or would it be completely different – somewhere else, doing something else? What would your future ideal self tell you to do?

If visualisation is not your strong suit, you can follow a process to work out what you do and don't like, and thus – at least roughly, the direction in which you would like to head. Firstly, make a list of anything you've done in your life that you really hated – I mean, seriously detested. Next, you must think carefully – were there any aspects of these jobs or situations that you liked? Or did you just hate absolutely everything about them? Write this all down on a blank piece of paper. An easy way to do this is to make a really simple table with 'loved' and 'hated' at the top, and a line down the middle to divide them. Then, make a list of anything that you loved or appreciated; or that made you feel positive or happy at any time. Consider things like whether you like being around people or prefer to work alone. Do you like being in a team that works collaboratively on a project, or do you prefer to be one-to-one and customer-facing? Is it something creative, or something very structured? Do you enjoy being around children, animals, or old people? Ask yourself all these questions, and any other related ones. If you're still unsure, speak to good friends, family, or colleagues. What do they think you're good at? When do you seem most engaged or knowledgeable?

You can use the same technique we talked about in chapter 3 in prioritising your life. Tal Ben-Shahar suggests to imagine that a spell of anonymity had been cast over your life. Nobody would ever know what you were doing ever again. What would you then choose to do?[87] This should really help you get to the bottom of who you are, independent from what other people think of you, or who you think you should be.

Looking back over my life, I came to realise that I'd actually given up on a lot of the things that I used to really enjoy and be quite passionate about. I stopped watching football because I didn't have anyone to share my passion with. Nobody in my household was interested, so I just quietly gave up. How many good things in life have been given up due to silly excuses, apathy, or active discouragement from people or the culture around you? It's not only important to (re)discover your passions, but also to realise what's stopping you from enjoying them as part of your life. It's all too easy to just give up

---

[87] Ben-Shahar, T. (2008) Ibid.

on things that truly make us happy. This happens predominantly due to major life changes, e.g. having a child, moving away, or changing jobs. We make excuses like: "we've got no time now"; "we've got kids"; "it's too far away"; or "it's too complicated". There are, in fact, many ways you can regain enjoyment from your passions. Perhaps you can't travel into the city anymore to go dancing in the evening, but you could organise or visit a local dance event in your village. Perhaps you can't have a dog in your apartment block, but you could volunteer to walk another person's dog. You could even tie this in with your greater-than-self goals and enjoy helping others as well as getting exercise and all the fun of a canine friend! Remember, don't limit yourself, but seek to find alternative ways of enjoying these things.

Hopefully, you should now have an idea of some of your passions and how you might be able to enjoy them according to your current life circumstances. Knowing that you will be able to work on something you're passionate about either every day or week, even if it is only for 10 minutes, will help you get out of bed in the morning already expecting great things to happen. You need to locate your inner child, the one that looks forward to every new day. Place on your nightstand the photo of your favourite activity planned for the day, so you see it when you wake up. It could be baking, DIY, reading, watching races, gardening, making bath bombs for pampering yourself and family... Anything that takes your fancy.

Would you like to volunteer but you don't think 10 minutes a day is enough? Think again – some charities or organisations such as youth clubs etc. would welcome someone to help respond to Tweets here and there, answer an email or call a person in need – you might even be responding to someone who might be in a similar situation to you. Alternatively, you might be able to help looking after a charity stall at the weekend, or bake a cake for their sale, or walk your elderly neighbour's dog when it's icy outside. Or are you passionate about painting? How about using your commute time to draw/paint or take a photo of something beautiful instead of checking your phone for the millionth time to see whether someone called, texted, or updated their Facebook page?

Let's stop for a second and consider technology in our lives. We have above two examples; the first one is deeply meaningful – using technology to support others, volunteer, etc. It helps you work on your passion and helps others create social context and the feeling of being valued and less isolated. However, as in the second example, this positive effect does not happen when we keep checking our phone and social media accounts for ourselves – only to see what others are up to and what a great (airbrushed) life they live. This just increases any stress and anxiety through 'fear of missing out' (FOMO) on all the parties, fun activities, and holidays others are enjoying. Unless used wisely for strengthening relationships and arranging face-to-face meetings, social media can perpetuate our perception that someone's life (heavily airbrushed for posting on their Facebook wall) is better than ours. Let's face it – unless loved ones need us to be on call at all times, checking phones and social media does not count as a productive use of time, especially if it makes you feel like someone else's life is more awesome than yours.

Gratefulness

Rather than being jealous, saddened, or experiencing serious FOMO, a more productive and beneficial use of our time is to practise gratefulness. Remember the child's bedtime routine from the last chapter? It included prayers. Now, I know some people are not interested in religion or spiritual matters, but the essence of night-time prayers, for me, is about gratefulness. Acknowledging the good things in our lives and being thankful for them is a deep and powerful practice. What helped me as a first step in the right direction was to switch off the news. Watching or listening to news didn't do anything good for me – especially last thing at night or first thing in the morning, because it set a negative and worried tone for my day. Yet, even though the news media is full of bad, negative, and downright horrible reports, the reality is that there is good in the world going on all the time, every day. It's just sad that we don't see it emblazoned across the news media. If we reminded ourselves regularly just how much good was happening around us, I believe we would live our lives quite differently and much more happily.

But don't just take my word for it, there is a proven, scientific reason for why gratefulness works. You see, when we search for something to be grateful for, it activates pathways in our brain that can increase dopamine and serotonin, two substances I mentioned when talking about happiness and motivation. Gratitude: "activates a brain stem region which is responsible for the production of dopamine".[88] In addition, if you are grateful to   more enjoyable through more activit   amine circuits. As for serotonin, practisir   focus on the positive aspects of your lif   otonin production."[89]

This simple practice can help   brief moments of attention. It develops our emotional intelligence and habituates our brain into 'search' mode, making us happier even

---

[88] Korb, A. (2015) Ibid.

[89] As above

before we've found a specific thing for which we're going to give thanks. Regularly looking for things to be grateful for (even when we don't find them) helps our brain sustain the pathway and still brings us the rewards of increased happiness through higher serotonin and dopamine production. You don't even have to be grateful for massive things. The secret to seeing the good in the world is first to acknowledge the good things in your own life: a beautiful flower or magnificent tree on your way to work; a full belly after dinner; or a child's simple, perfect smile. I love how it is succinctly described here on www.gratefulness.org (a great website to check out!):

> "Grateful living is a way of life which asks us to notice all that is already present and abundant – from the tiniest things of beauty to the grandest of our blessings – and in so doing, to take nothing for granted. We can learn to focus our attention on, and acknowledge, that life is a gift. Even in the most challenging times, living gratefully makes us aware of, and available to, the opportunities that are always available; opportunities to learn and grow, and to extend ourselves with care and compassion to others. Grateful living is based in, and reinforces, values such as respect, responsibility, and generosity. Small, grateful acts every day can uplift us, make a difference for others, and help change the world."[90]

Can you see a running theme here? Those mindfulness core abilities of awareness and focus are cropping up again. It seems that happiness, gratefulness, and mindfulness are very much intertwined.

---

[90] Gratefulness.org (2015). Mission, vision and values. Retrieved January 30, 2017, from http://www.gratefulness.org/about/values-mission-vision/

I have no idea which one comes first; perhaps it's a chicken-and-egg situation?

Gratefulness might not come to you naturally, if you find yourself 'in the deep end' and most of your life seems like a struggle with terrible things that have happened. Perhaps worries about the future or reprimands keep popping up uninvited in your head. But this is exactly the best time to start. I saw this in myself. In the last few years, gratefulness didn't come as naturally to me as it did when I was younger. I kept looking into the past at my failures and pain – what I couldn't do anymore, and I moped about when my best friend moved to another country. But I decided I needed to make a change; I didn't want to lead a miserable existence. I wanted to be happy and I wanted other people to feel content, joyful and cared for in my presence. I realised that I needed to introduce a bit more positivity and happiness into my life and I started with the simple things. I started my 'news-media-free' life and a written gratefulness journal challenge. Every night, instead of watching or reading about the news online, I wrote down 3 simple things for which I was grateful.

There are simple things in my journal – like it not raining when I have to bike down to the shop to fetch milk; the sunny walk to work in the morning; my daughter admiring a ladybug (from a safe distance); hot water running anytime of the day (not the case at my parent's place); a comfy bed on holidays, etc. I became much more focussed on the reality of my life, rather than what someone else wanted me to know and think about. Just significantly reducing my TV viewing in general really helped me to focus on the important things in my life. I don't truly care about which idiot politicians were shouting at each other this week, or which Z-list 'celebrity' did something unmentionable (which apparently needs mentioning on the news) that nobody really cares about.

Once you start practising gratefulness for more things in your life, your overall level of happiness will improve. This study[91] showed that students who chose to take part in improving wellbeing through practising gratitude and positive visualisation, reported higher levels of wellbeing and increases in happiness even 6 months after the study had finished. These students were successful in increasing their happiness, because they chose to practise and they found the right way to do so. Thanks to their efforts, their happiness and wellbeing measures increased. The main message was, however, that for the intervention to work, **there needs to be will and the effort** put into it.

Moreover, Seligman[92] researched five additional positive exercises (practised over 1 week) that were thought to increase happiness among an online sample of participants. One of the things this study showed was that those who spent time each day to consider three **good** things that happened to them showed increases in their happiness and declines in their depressive symptoms over a period of 6 months or longer. Imagine that – after just one week of practice! An increase in happiness and decrease in depression was also markedly noticeable in participants who wrote and delivered a **letter of gratitude**.

Why don't you have a go at it too – as a challenge?

---

[91] Lyubomirsky, S., Dickerhoof, R., Boehm, J. K., & Sheldon, K. M. (2011). Becoming happier takes both a will and a proper way: An experimental longitudinal intervention to boost well-being. *Emotion*, *11*(2), 391–402. doi:10.1037/a0022575

[92] Seligman, M. (2005) Ibid.

Challenge one: Try writing a gratitude journal. If you do this in the morning, you will positive *and* you will have accomplished something good, first thing.

Challenge two: Positive visualisation of the best possible future self.[93] I mentioned your ideal future self earlier in this book; this is one way you can work on visualisation: think about a specific situation or topic in the future (next year, in five years etc.) and imagine that everything has gone as well as it could have. Write about it. It could be any topic e.g. your romantic life/marriage, education, career, family, health and wellbeing, mental health, hobbies, social life, or volunteering.

Challenge three: Expressing gratitude through writing a letter to a specific recipient.[94] Think about a situation in your life when you felt grateful to someone – why, and how did this person affect your life? Why do you appreciate them? Then write about it as if you were going to send them a thank-you letter. An adaptation on this would be a thank-you email that you could send to a friend or a person to whom you are grateful. Try to write a letter or a note each week for 8 weeks to a partner, friend, parent, teacher, colleague, neighbour, etc.

---

[93] King, L. A. (2001). The health benefits of writing about life goals. *Personality and Social Psychology Bulletin, 27*(7), 798–807. doi:10.1177/0146167201277003

[94] Emmons, R. A., & McCullough, M. E. (2003). Counting blessings versus burdens: An experimental investigation of gratitude and subjective well-being in daily life. *Journal of Personality & Social Psychology, 84*(2), 377–389. doi:10.1037//0022-3514.84.2.377

You can try to follow challenges two and three for 8 weeks,[95] or you can choose a timeframe that suits you. You will see after an attempt or two whether you enjoy the challenge and how it makes you feel. You will also find that the longer you practise, the better your brain will become at it and in the end, and you won't even need to write anything down. Your brain will release dopamine and serotonin when you begin thinking about gratitude. Just remember, there needs to be will and effort put into any practice to reap the most benefits.[96]

Growing and challenging yourself – motivate yourself like an athlete

Now, we know it's not all about your brain and we have already talked a little about the effect stress has on your body. You need to build resilience on both fronts – mental as well as physical. Now that you (hopefully) know what makes you tick, you can work at becoming more like those athletes we discussed earlier. I'm not saying you're going to become the next Serena Williams or Usain Bolt, but you can certainly enhance your own life. You can tap into that powerful and amazing brain and body of yours, allowing yourself to grow and develop an athletic mindset as well as growing your fitness. You can do this by challenging yourself physically through exercise, walking, hiking, etc. But also mentally, by gradually exposing yourself to situations that are brand new or that you know make you feel anxious or stressed.

Let's learn to face our fears and practise our new, flexible mindset!

---

[95] as done in the study by Lyubomirsky, S. et al., (2011) Ibid.

[96] As above

If you're a little bit anxious about public speaking, you can practise mental exercises like closing your eyes and imagining that you are in a public place where you're meant to speak. Imagine the situation, the people around you and your bodily reactions, and keep repeating to yourself that this is an exciting challenge from which you will grow and learn. Observe curiously, and with kindness, what is happening in your body. Remember your mindfulness techniques. Your body is not betraying you! Your brain and body are learning to work together through an exciting challenge; you are in a safe place, after all, it's just imaginary. You can withstand this and gradually lengthen the time before you open your eyes.

If you are worried about panic attacks, please speak to your medical professional about the suitability of graded exposure therapy and possibly practising it under supervision.

Try something new and continue learning. Continued learning develops your flexibility, in coping as well as in acquiring and using new information. It keeps you mentally sharp well into old age and helps you cope with stressful situations. Try to learn or do something new every day; and whatever ritual you have or activity that makes you happy, try to keep it fresh with little variations and surprises. It will help keep you interested and happier for longer, staving off hedonic adaptation. After all, the paper on how to sustain happiness increases and prevents hedonic adaptation was called **Variety is the Spice of Happiness**: The Hedonic adaptation prevention (HAP) model.[97]

---

[97] Sheldon, K. M., Boehm, J., & Lyubomirsky, S. (2015, April 13). Variety is the spice of happiness: The Hedonic adaptation prevention model. Retrieved January 30, 2017, from

As for the physical challenges, think of any type of exercise or physical activity. Yes, exercise helps you become fit, but there's more to it. If you are anxious and worried about the physical effects of stress, anxiety, or panic on your body (sweating, fast heartbeat or breathing), exercise enables you to gradually tolerate these physical signs in a safe way. You will become more accustomed to these physical effects over time, thus decreasing the fear created by future stressful or anxiety-inducing situations.[98]

So, in other words, the more you expose your body to the physical signs of stress, the more your body will be used to these symptoms. Consequently, you will find the emotions and thoughts you experience when you are next under high-stress conditions less alarming. Remember, fast heartbeat and breathing, as well as sweating, are your body's signs that it is preparing to meet the challenge. These experiences, e.g. skydiving, can be exciting or worrying depending on how you see them. They are also the signs of your body being able to handle exercise and getting ready to produce endorphins that make you happy; and last, but not least, exercise boosts serotonin, making it a perfect threefold action.

This may seem a bit too simple, however there is a slight 'but' in this. To get the most out of your exercise (and any other activity that you're doing to boost your serotonin levels), *you need to make a conscious and free choice.* You need to decide that you *want* and *love* to do it, not that you should, ought to, or must. If you feel forced to exercise, as if it's a chore, you have not made a voluntary choice and your brain knows this. You will therefore receive a lower dopamine

---

http://www.oxfordhandbooks.com/view/10.1093/oxfordhb/9780199557257.001.0001/oxfordhb-9780199557257-e-067

[98] Southwick, S. M. & Charney, D. S. (2012). Ibid.

boost (Alex Korb, The upward spiral). However, if you perceive yourself as an exercise junkie and you love it, you will get a bigger hit of dopamine. The more you love it and are excited about doing it, the better effect it will have.

This is similar to the act of being generous with your time or means (money). When participants in a study at the University of Oregon[99] received cash, and were asked whether they wanted to donate some of this money to a food bank, some said yes. Interestingly, their brain's reward centre activated the release of dopamine. They received a bigger dopamine boost if they chose to do this voluntarily, rather than when researchers took some of their money away without permission, to donate on the participants' behalf. So, the choice is yours as to whether exercising, being generous, or any other activities will give you a bigger or smaller happiness boost. Do you choose to feel like these things are forced upon you, or do you choose to see them as activities you love and enjoy?

Do you not feel like making a choice to be a happy bunny and exercise? What if you just don't feel like going out and doing something today? Why not just wait until you feel like exercising or until you feel you have the time or money to give? Well, I hate to break it to you, but you might be feeling low exactly because you aren't doing those things yet. You might have low levels of serotonin and dopamine. Waiting for them to appear out of thin air won't help.

---

[99] Harbaugh, W. T., Mayr, U., & Burghart, D. R. (2007). Neural responses to taxation and voluntary giving reveal motives for charitable donations. *Science*, *316*(5831), 1622–1625. doi:10.1126/science.1140738

Sometimes you need to pick yourself up and do something good in order to feel good.

I do understand, that it is sometimes difficult to drum up enthusiasm and love for mundane actions and tasks (exercise is just one of many possible examples) and things that you simply must do in order to pay the bills, keep fit (despite pain or lack of time), and go through the motions to make an acceptable living. Putting aside the discussion about what is acceptable to me or others, remember 'job crafting' from chapter 1? The principle is the same. Go back to the list of the tasks you do daily and really think about those that are annoying; those you hate; or those that you simply ought to do, but don't like doing. You need to remind yourself of their value in your life and what they really mean. Remind yourself why you love doing them! Try the worksheet: "4.1 Meaning and Value Every Day". Remember, all the worksheets are accessible via www.ruskinpublishing.co.uk/titles/.

For example, I feel that I need to exercise. It never felt like a chore until I started suffering from chronic pain. Now, I feel weak and awkward in the gym, so I have avoided some types of exercise. I have become gradually less fit, and I am feeling even more awkward about going back to the gym because I haven't been for so long. But I know from experience that if I do go, I feel great afterwards (as long as I don't overdo it) and nobody looks at me strangely! So, in my head, I need to rephrase this whole experience to make it work for me. I want to be fit for my children, so I can keep up with them – take them swimming or cycling, etc. I don't want to be excluded from any of these activities. And I don't want to miss out on any fun we have as a family.

My mental exercise (you can try it too) was:

Meaning of exercise: mood boost, able to run after my toddler and lift her comfortably, stop the deconditioning and getting fit for my later years (there's no point feeling 55 when I'm only 35).

My new mantra is:

"I love exercise! It makes me happy and makes me fit, so I can be an awesome mum and can keep up with the kids as well as adults in the future, without missing out on any of their fun. Plus, when I retire, I can look forward to being fit and healthy and enjoy travelling again, without the kids – yay!"

You may need to consider tweaking slightly what you need to do to make it more 'you' or more convenient. I decided to get a cross trainer for home so that I don't have to make childcare arrangements if I want to do a five-minute exercise every morning. Plus, I don't have to feel awkward about exercising in my pyjamas. It's a win-win situation, and it makes me happy to get up in the morning, knowing I can do something for myself that is not only making me stronger physically, but also mentally. You can do this with any 'should do' item on your list with the help of my "2.6 Should, Ought to, and Must" worksheet.

However, you don't have to go to the gym or even get a piece of equipment to be able to start exercising at home. You can follow videos with yoga or Pilates exercises on YouTube. You can walk, lift light weights (try lifting canned foods or a couple of large books), do energetic cleaning or dancing in the shower. Whatever you do – and there are many activities you can choose from, do it with love and enthusiasm to get the most benefit.

Exercise is amazing, because it gives back more than it takes!

Motivation for physical as well as mental challenges

Remember: if you make it a habit or a ritual, it will be much easier to maintain; but what other ways are there to help you get going? We have mentioned a couple already:

Plan it!

Employ your prefrontal cortex, make a specific plan, make it visible, set yourself reminders, and address any possible obstacles ahead of time – use sentences such as: 'If (x happens) then I will':

- If it rains, then I will go swimming instead of running;

- If I miss the bus, then I will do core exercises at home;

- If the class is cancelled, then I will text my friend or another participant to arrange a meet up to practise separately;

- If I am too tired, then I will go for a brisk morning walk instead of watching the news.

Make it into a game

Have fun – create a wall chart you can fill in with your achievements or simple tick boxes. Give yourself stars and rewards for your achievements (3 in a row, 5 in a row, etc.). You can also engage your family members or friends for support as well as accountability. You can agree with a buddy to text each other every day with your achievements and cheer each other on, or you could compete with your children or partner. The person with a longer streak of successes at the end of the week could have control over: the remote control;

what to cook for dinner; a games night; etc. Or collect points over a longer time – let's say three months – and promise yourself a big reward if you collect X amount of points. However, you need to be realistic over how much you can achieve or how many times you are allowed to miss.

Connect the activities you need to do with those you love

If you don't really enjoy walking, but you need to do it (for health reasons or pure lack of transport), then attach it to something you love. Listen to your favourite music or podcast, ask a friend to join you for a walk, take a camera and photograph interesting things (picture-a-day challenge?), or explore geocaching – a modern take on treasure hunts.

Consider the end

Often, imagining beginning a new thing is much worse than doing it. Imagining going to the gym could leave you feeling intimidated; it could remind you of the pain you may (or may not actually) feel, how sweaty you will be, etc. So, the answer is not to stay at home, but rather to imagine how it will feel after you've been to the gym. You will have achieved your plan and goal, so you will be on a serotonin and dopamine high. Feeling happy, accomplished, less anxious or stressed, and becoming fitter.

You can also use these strategies to motivate yourself to do anything you find a struggle – from household chores, to socialising, getting through family get-togethers, taking exams, or starting a new course, school, job, etc.

By bringing your focus to the right things, you will be able to manage your day-to-day life with ease. Your emotional resilience will increase through the practices found in this chapter, and you should find yourself growing and becoming more capable over time. It's important to try and keep track of these changes, so that they always remain at the forefront of your mind as a conscious choice and practice. We recommend journalling a few lines every night as a helpful practice, which can be revisited after a few weeks and months. You will notice the changes in your life as you put your energy into the various suggestions I have made.

Summary of Chapter 4:

• Relationships disarm stress effects through caring, helping, listening and releasing oxytocin.

• The 'tend and befriend' response activates oxytocin as well as dopamine and serotonin.

• Socialising helps us live longer, lowers cholesterol and helps against depression and isolation.

• Use your interests and passions to create social networks.

• You can use mindful awareness to focus on the present and be realistic.

• Compassion to self and others helps us battle isolation – it's a necessity, not a luxury.

• Increasing your happiness increases your success.

• Challenges, learning, and variety keep you sharp, resilient, and happy in the long term.

• Physical exercise – whatever you do, CHOOSE to do it and LOVE it to get the most benefit.

Afterword:

Thank you very much for reading my book to the end. I sincerely hope that it was easier reading than it was writing (it was a massive learning curve for me!) and that the research and experience I have shared with you will encourage you to explore new ways of thinking about your life, stress, and a new mindset to tackle both.

If you've gained anything from reading this book, it would be *really helpful* if you could take a moment and **leave a review on Amazon**. It will hopefully aid others in finding this book, and offer them an alternative way forward through the stresses of everyday life.

There is more information about me on **www.ruskinpublishing.co.uk** where you can also find your **free printable materials**, if you have not yet accessed them. Hopefully, they have made it easier to incorporate some of the ideas mentioned in this book into your life. Please let me know what you thought of them and whether they were helpful.

If you have any feedback at all, good or bad, or if you would like to tell me about your experience of making these ideas part of your life, please reach out to me via **SHansen@ruskinpublishing.co.uk**. I would love to hear from you. I will read all messages and do my best to reply to you as soon as I can.

Thank you again for staying with me till the end. I really appreciate you and hope that this is the start of something great for you!

Sara Hansen

30819813R00089

Printed in Poland
by Amazon Fulfillment
Poland Sp. z o.o., Wrocław